Perennial Classics:

Planting & Growing
Great Perennial Gardens

Easy-Growing Gardening Guide, Vol. 4

Melinda R. Cordell

Although the author has made every effort to ensure that the information in this book was correct at press time, the author does not assume and hereby disclaims any liability to any party for any loss, damage, or disruption caused by errors or omissions, whether such errors or omissions result from space aliens, evil imps, your kids, somebody else's kids, man-eating Venus flytraps, running out of coffee in the morning, the Flying Spaghetti Monster, that thing when you walk into a room and you can't remember what you came in there for, ticks, outraged mallards, or any other cause.

ISBN: 154537225X
ISBN-13: 978-1545372258

**For more information (and books!), visit
www.melindacordell.com**

ALL THE BOOKS I'VE WRITTEN
SO FAR

Civil War Books
Courageous Women of the Civil War: Soldiers, Spies, Medics, and More (Chicago Review Press, 2016)
Gentlemen, Accept This Facial Hair Challenge! Epic Beards and Moustaches of the Civil War

Young Adult Novels
Angel in the Whirlwind
Butterfly Chaos
Those Black Wings

The Easy-Growing Gardening Series
Don't Throw in the Trowel: Vegetable Gardening Month by Month
Rose to the Occasion: An Easy-Growing Guide to Rose Gardening
If You're a Tomato, I'll Ketchup With You: Tomato Gardening Tips and Tricks
Perennial Classics: Planting and Growing Great Perennial Gardens

Forthcoming Middle Grade Novels:
Outlander's Scar
Wandering Stars
Silverlady

CONTENTS

INTRODUCTION
WHY ARE PERENNIALS HARD TO BEAT?

When I was in college, I hit a rough patch and had to drop out. I was working two part-time jobs while taking full-time classes, paying for rent, food, and college (I had no financial aid), while living on ramen and hot dogs. (Fun fact: Due to my poverty diet, the iron levels in my blood were so low that I was not allowed to give blood.) Also, I kept wanting to change majors – I wanted to be an English major, but I kept being told that I needed to get a major that I could earn money in. "You can't make a living out of writing books." So I came back home and started living in my old hometown of Nodaway, and I got a job at a garden center.

I had a great boss and co-workers at the garden center. We worked with the annuals, perennials, and herbs. We would sing while grooming the plants (when I say "grooming the plants," I mean picking the dead leaves and old flowers off the plants – we weren't brushing the plants' hair or anything). We had a lot of good stuff to talk about, and we helped customers find what they wanted, and when they had gardening questions and we didn't know the answers, we'd do everything we could to find the answer. It was a great deal.

The nice thing about working at a garden center is that you get a lot of free plants. Every day you'd work through the flats and pots, and if you saw any plants that were dying or droopy or looked bad, you'd take them out. Some of them just needed a little tender loving care, so those would go to the "plant hospital," as we called it, where they would get a little attention and to perk up. Some of these would recover enough to go back on the tables, but some just sat there looking mopey, so we got to take these home.

I had a bit of a garden where I lived, but now I had a lot of garden. I wasn't very interested in annuals, because they were there for a season and that was it for them. But I loved the perennials. After all these years, I'm trying to put my finger on why they appealed so much to me. I think it was because everybody grew the same annuals over and over – marigolds, geraniums, petunias – but perennials weren't as common. I always go for stuff that's a little uncommon.

Another part of it was that some of these perennials could be true heirlooms in the garden, growing for years and years. I really wanted to grow a Gas Plant (*Dictamnus albus*) because they could stay alive for decades. Alas, the ones we had were just not in very good shape, and I didn't have much luck getting them started in my garden.

At the time, too, I was a little tired of the sameness of all the annuals. Granted, I would change my mind later, when I was working as a city horticulturist, because annuals were such a help in coloring up my flower beds fast. But give me a break, I was in college, and at that time I was just a teeny bit pretentious. Okay, more than a teeny bit.

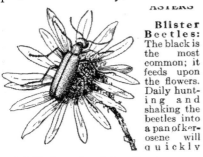

ASTERS
Blister Beetles: The black is the most common; it feeds upon the flowers. Daily hunting and shaking the beetles into a pan of kerosene will quickly

I also loved the variety of perennials. I had some Connecticut Blue delphiniums that bloomed in the most gorgeous shades of blue I'd ever seen in a plant. I had a Japanese anemone that was a whirligig of white flowers until a bunch of blister beetles ate it up. The jerks. Sea thrift, with its little powderpuff flowers growing out of a tuft of grass; Nepeta, or catmint, with its purple flowers. My cat was nuts about catnip, but she had no interest whatsoever in catmint. I planted some dahlia tubers and got some fascinating, gigantic flowers. A perennial hibiscus startled me with magenta flowers as big as dinner plates. Grandma Mary wanted to know what these plants were! And she is wise in all things plant, so that's saying something.

Now, bringing home a bunch of random plants from the nursery doesn't exactly make for an orderly garden. But I didn't care. I loved most the anticipation – of putting this sad, sickly little plant in the ground and giving it good soil and watering it regularly, and generally the plant would perk up and start growing, and the next year it would start flowering, and whoa! So that's what the flowers look like in real life! And it all started with a sad-looking little droopy twig.

That's one of the really cool things about perennials. They can fill a number of roles in the garden. You can get them in a variety of shapes, forms, and colors – whether they're chunky or elegant, variegated or colorful leaves, sprawling stems or upright, billowing and carefree or architecturally perfect. Perennials grow in all kinds of conditions, whether it's shade, desert, heat, or cold, and build the background of beautiful borders. Perennials can provide four-season beauty, and they grow stronger by the season. Perennials promise all these things – and they deliver.

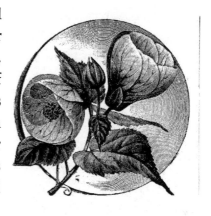

At the end of the spring season, when things were slowing down, I was hanging around the garden center one day with my boss and co-worker, just talking. I said, "You know what? I think I'm going to go back to school. And this time, I'm going to major in horticulture. You guys want to come with me?"

"Sure!" they said.

We ended up commuting to school together and took horticulture classes together, and I finally graduated four years later, or close enough. (I minored in writing, naturally.) So, again, perennials turned out to be very helpful. I did my senior thesis on English gardens and totally snowed my Senior Studies professor. He was an Ag man who didn't know much about gardening, so I got an A.

Shortly thereafter, I got a job as city horticulturist. I had a million gardens to plant in the spring. I planted annuals everywhere, but boy, that repetitive motion really hurt my hands and wrists. I used a trowel. Then I tried using bulb planters, which were not effective in the clayey soils in city gardens. Finally I used a little child's shovel to dig a series of holes, then dropped the annuals in and covered them up, in order to save my hands and wrists from all that digging. But this was a lot of labor in spring, and I was always so far behind on all the tasks that needed tending to.

So that fall, I bought a bunch of cheap perennials (everything goes on sale in the fall), wrote down the colors and blooming times for them so I could sort out what would look best where, and then I put them in various gardens to fill out the borders. A one-time planting saved a lot of time and trouble in the spring. Once the perennials filled out and started doing their thing, I didn't have to plant so many annuals, which eased my workload. Now I could do all the other things that needed done, which I couldn't do before because I had been planting annuals.

Oh, and I was a one-woman crew for the whole city. I was assigned inmate labor, but I couldn't send them off by themselves to work on other gardens – too bad. Or I'd get somebody doing community service, which was more of a babysitting job – decidedly unhelpful! At least in the summer I had a very helpful seasonal worker, and how I wish I could have had her working with me in early spring and early fall. But you can't have everything, I suppose.

I had perennials going in everywhere, even in the rose garden, for extra color and to give me an easier time in general. The nice thing was, in fall I could divide the perennials, then plant them out and have many more perennials. I could gather the seeds in October and November, when I was cleaning up the gardens, and plant them in the greenhouse to spread around the parks next spring. Your taxpayer dollars at work.

Anyway, this is why I am such a big fan of perennials. In recent years, roses have pretty much eclipsed perennials for me, These days, I'm starting to come back around to perennials again. They're easy to take care of, they offer a multitude of forms and shapes and sizes and colors and blooming times, and once they're in the ground, they're pretty good about growing for a long time. They got me into my major in college (finally), they saved me a lot of time as a horticulturist, and they look good. All in all, a very, very helpful kind of plant to have.

This book will show you around this fascinating world of perennials. I'll show you how to figure out what you need in your garden by looking at what your garden has to offer your plants in terms of site, the amount of sunlight and rain it gets, and ways to improve the soil for best results. I'll talk about garden design (because with perennials, you work with not only color, but coordinating bloom times for all-season color), how to care for your perennials, how to keep them looking good through the year, and ways to troubleshoot your garden problems, whether it's insect pests, diseases, animals, or weeds.

Welcome aboard!

Hey, if you have any ideas for future books, or see something I've missed in this book that you'd like to see covered, drop me a line at rosefiend@gmail.com and I'll get right on it. Also, if you want to subscribe to my newsletter, go to my website at melindacordell.com and sign up, and you'll always know when my next book will be coming out. You can also help me choose upcoming topics, book covers, etc., and I'll give you free chapters, book samples, and gardening tips. Enjoy!

Now, back to the book.

FIRST STEPS IN PERENNIAL GARDENING

What the heck are perennials, anyway?

If you go by the dictionary definition, perennials are hardy herbaceous ornamental plants. That is, they have green growth (not woody growth like trees or shrubs), and they survive your local winters to come back year after year, and they look good in the garden. In the winter, they'll die back to the ground so just about all the above-ground growth is dead, but in spring they grow back up from the roots and bloom again. And every year they grow and change, so in the perennial garden, you always have something new happening. Barbara Damrosch in *The Garden Primer* (a book I recommend highly) says, "The garden is not a set piece but a process." Technically, that's a good description of any garden, when you think about it.

Annuals will die off every winter, but perennials survive the cold. However, annuals will bloom their heads off from spring until fall, and keep going until a frost turns them black and you have to pull them up. Perennials have a specific blooming time every year, from one week to up to a month. Some will rebloom if you cut them back at the right time, such as black-eyed Susans or chrysanthemums.

Perennials come in all shapes, sizes, and can be grown in just about any biome in the world. (Not *every* biome, as it would be extremely challenging to grow a perennial garden in Antarctica. However, with global warming as it is, this will not be the case for long.)

When I said a garden evolves, that includes the perennial garden. Some plants will do very well in your yard. Some might not. Some will need divided every few years to keep them healthy and vigorous. You might take out some that you're not crazy about and replace them with those you love. Or you notice that most of your plants bloom only in spring or fall, but not enough of them bloom in the summer, so you need to fit in some summer-blooming plants to bring in some flowers in July and August.

You might keep tucking perennials into your flower bed – but that's okay, because many plants are actually social beings, and they like to sit close to each other. This seems strange, but when you look at plants in the wild, are they spaced out? or are they all jumbled together? Let your garden reflect your plants' natural habitat and natural growth habits – and you get healthier, merrier plants.

Perennials generally live longer than three years. Some perennials are short-lived – Shasta daisies and flax are two examples of perennials that die after a year or two. However, some, like peonies, gas plants, and hostas, can live for decades.

SELECTING YOUR GARDEN SITE

If you're a beginner, start small. You can always make the garden bed bigger if you are really crazy about gardening. If your interest wanes – or if some unexpected life event comes up that makes taking care of your garden difficult – then the garden is still manageable. It's easier to expand a garden than to make it smaller. Also, gardening is easier if you're not overwhelmed by it. Trust me.

When you are placing your garden, don't forget to put it in a place where you can see and enjoy it. Look through your kitchen window, consider the view from your deck or upstairs window. If you can place it where you can easily look out and enjoy it, you're in business. Bonus points if you can place the garden close enough to a window so you can plant a fragrant rose right there and enjoy the scent.

If you're just starting out, you'll need to figure out what your garden spot has to offer. Is it a shady spot or sunny, or a mix of both? To better understand what that area provides, look at the plants growing there right now.

If you see a bunch of lush grass growing thickly in the sun, that tells you that that this is a full-sun location with fertile soil. If you see ground ivy or English ivy, or grass that's sparse because of the shade, then use that area for a shade garden. If there's nothing growing there because the shade is too dense, you'd better find another spot for your plants, or trim off some limbs to let in some more light. Use your observations to find the best plants for the site. Some perennials love full sun all day – some love the shade – some can take a bit of both.

Also, look at how much water the area gets. Does water linger in puddles here long after a rain? Or, does it seem that you can never water this area enough because the soil is so sandy? You can fix clay soils and sandy soils by adding compost. If your soil is especially problematic, install raised beds and fill them with potting soil and compost, then plant.

Check the drainage of the soil. Dig a hole six inches deep. Fill it with water. If the water drains away within the hour, then you have good drainage. If not – or if the water won't drain hardly at all – then you might consider installing raised beds for your perennials. (Note: Obviously, if you've already had a ton of rain, or if it's flood season, this test won't be much good.)

If you do have a puddly place in the place where you're dead set on having a garden, you can either fill in the hole with some good compost, or make the best of a bad situation by putting a birdbath, small water feature, or even make a mud puddle for butterflies to drink at and add in some butterfly garden features there.

As you've making notes, look at the slope. Ideally, the ground should slope from the middle of the garden down to the front, so that water will not puddle right in the middle of your garden.

If you are planting on the side of a hill, consider how to set up the garden to keep erosion to a minimum. I don't know if you've heard of terrace farming, but it's a kind of way farmers set up their field to keep erosion to a minimum. There are no uphill or downhill lines in these fields – only horizontal lines, or furrows, or terraces. Follow the same setup in your garden, setting it from one side of the slope to the other, instead of going straight down the slope.

If the slope is very bad, groundcovers are a possibility. If you are a determined sort, an alpine garden would be a possibility here, so you still can have your perennials AND you will have good erosion control, and one less slope to mow (and fall down). So there is that.

If you're planning to take out those old yews and barberries, or whatever shrubs were put in for foundation plantings, be prepared for a little heavy work. Digging out an old yew takes a lot of digging, to get down under the roots far enough to cut it out. When I was working in landscape installation, there was one particularly large yew that just would not come out. We'd dug a hole that was a good three feet wide and the roots were wide and thick. I believe a pickax was involved in this operation, various saws, and even then we had about three people rocking the stump back and forth. We'd lean it as hard as possible to the right, and try to saw out what roots we could get from that angle, then we'd lean it hard to the left and repeat the operation.

Finally we managed to wrest that thing out of there and there was celebration all around, and possibly some after-work beers, which were more than well-deserved. So, in short, yew bushes can be a bear to deal with. If you're buff and tough, and you don't mind a lot of digging, AND you have a good quality saw, then knock yourself out. (Not literally – I hope.) Otherwise, hire a contractor to do this.

Measuring your yard.

Find a couple of sheets of graph paper for your design. Then measure out your house. The easiest way is to get a measuring wheel (also called a surveyor's wheel, a clickwheel, hodometer, or trundle wheel) at the local hardware store. A good-quality one will cost more, but I used a portable one with a tiny wheel and a number ticker on it. The handle telescoped down so you could stow it in the toolbox. This wheel turned out to be the one I used most, since I always had it handy in the city truck.

You can start with a plain sheet of paper, jotting down the measurements as you go. Start with the house, the garage, outbuildings, driveway, sidewalks, decks, the placement of trees and shrubs on the property, the patio, etc.

Now, keep in mind that you should measure the whole yard ONLY if you are undertaking a large project. If you are fixing to just plant a small bed along the side of the house, don't worry about the whole rest of the yard. There's no using in driving yourself to distraction when you don't need it!

While you're walking around measuring everything, take note of the conditions in the place where you want to plant. How does the sun look here? are you getting any shade where you are? Sometimes one assumes certain ideas about an area of the yard – until you actually spend some time there.

If you don't want to plant next to the house, consider a border along a fence or your sidewalk. Another possibility is an island bed in the middle of your lawn, perhaps tied to one of your trees.

Also, consider the backdrop of your flower bed. If you have a nice wall to place it against, or a picket fence, consider putting it there, to give some visual contrast to your flowers, and also to give the design an anchor. A row of evergreens or a tidy hedge is also nice. If you go with an island bed, you can have a tree in the center or on one side or the other, in order to provide height, color, and an anchor in the visual composition of the design. If you are planting next to a wall, building, or fence, put some space between the plants and the structure. First, this allows air to circulate behind the plants and helps to keep plant diseases like powdery mildew, blackspot, or other fungal diseases down. Also, a space behind the border allows you to squeeze back there and clean up the plants and keep up with maintenance, which is also important to plant health, and of course to the overall look of the plant border. A three-foot space is ideal so you don't get tangled up in your own plants.

How wide should the border be?

Getting in and around the border is very important. If you make the border too wide or large, it's going to be tough to maintain. Generally, a border that is two to three feet wide works just fine. If you have a dedicated gardener – or if you *are* a dedicated gardener – the old-fashioned English perennial borders were about six to eight feet wide, which allowed you to put in all those plants of all heights and sizes, with big plants at the back and smaller plants in the front, and allowed for nearly continuous bloom.

Now some folks get really excited about gardening and eventually end up with a yard full of garden, with little paths winding here and there and all kinds of cool flowers, shrubs, trees. Don't be discouraged if you can't attain this level of gardentude. Whatever you can maintain comfortably is best.

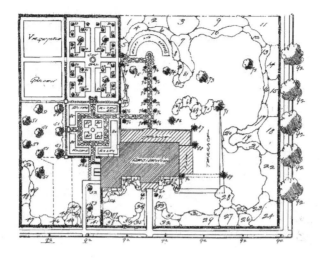

ELEMENTS OF DESIGN IN THE PERENNIAL GARDEN

A Garden is Never Finished – It Simply Evolves

The problem with gardening (or, the very interesting thing about gardening) is that you are dealing with living beings. Obviously these living beings can't communicate in the way we think of communication, and they can't run away or swat the trowel out of your hand when you dig too close to their roots. Nevertheless, plants are living beings, which means they have certain whims and they definitely have ideas of their own, and they most assuredly will do their own thing. So bear this in mind when you plant what you expect is a perfect border and then the plants all sit there and make faces at you (metaphorically speaking, of course).

A garden is never finished – it keeps evolving. The short-lived plants will die out and be replaced, some plants get divided or moved around; new plants and fashions will come and go, or you'll run across some new varieties that you have to try. At any rate, the garden always changes. Even if you make a lovely plan on paper, it's still a rough draft. The garden is the final copy.

… though, in truth, you can never say that "the garden is the final copy" because the garden itself keeps evolving as well. Even if you never add anything else to the garden, the plants themselves will keep growing and blooming (or die), and some will reseed themselves with a vengeance. Of course the weeds will have their day whether you want them to or not. So even if you do nothing but maintain a garden, it will keep changing – will never be the same from one year to the next.

And besides, perennials are always moveable. If you find they don't work in one location, then dig them up and move them to a new place. Divide some of them and share 'em with your grandma, or your gardening buddies.

I just said "perennials are moveable," but as always, the rule has exceptions. Plants with long taproots, like gas plant (Dictamnus) and indigo (Baptisia) aren't very happy about being moved, and will mope when you transplant them. On the whole, however, perennials are fairly cool about being dug up and moved around. Plants are generally tougher than you think they are. And if they do croak, well, get one that's tougher.

My motto as horticulturist was, "If it doesn't want to grow, well, then, it can just go away someplace and wilt." I didn't have time to baby my plants. They had to take care of themselves. You figure out pretty quickly what plants are tough and what plants are wimps. Fortunately, there are a ton of very good, easy-growing plants out there.

Don't sweat your garden plan. Nothing is perfect

So if you're sweating about making a perfect plan, don't. I include this information about creating a landscape plan to help you – but in this end, this is your garden. Some gardeners are "pantsers" – that is, they fly by the seats of their pants. "Hey, here are some flats of cosmos on sale – let's stick 'em in the garden! Well, there's no real good place for them, so we'll cram them behind the yarrow and let them fight it out."

When I first had a garden during my college interregnum, I generally had one plant of whatever leftovers I had from work, and that was my garden. I considered it my learning garden. I certainly was not going to invite any gardening clubs out to see it. I was having fun on my limited budget – and that limited budget ended up going to my college anyway, when I started going back for my horticulture degree. Them's the breaks!

So if a design right now seems like too much work, then skip it. Or draw a very loose sketch.

When I first started working with the city, I drew landscape plans for my gardens in winter. But when spring rolled around, I'd find that, for one reason or another, the plans always fell apart. Another garden would use up all the plants intended for another garden. There'd be a case of damping-off disease that would wipe out the trays of marigolds meant for City Hall. Or I'd see the colors together and say, "Ick," and swap out the offending plants for something better.

After a while, I gave up drawing plans. I had a general idea of what I wanted in each garden, anyway. I wrote down the colors and bloom times of the perennials and other plants already in the garden. Then, when it was time to plant, I'd go into the greenhouse and see what I had available. "Felix

Street Square has Nepeta, Perovskia, and Armeria on the northwest side, and the Billy Baffin roses (actually, this was William Baffin, but I was very casual with this rose). Pink and purple all over the place. Let's grab three flats of the magenta vincas. How do the pink geraniums look with the – whoa, those colors are actually vibrating, put 'em back. You'd think they'd match better than that. Hey, I forgot about the Ageratum hiding over there, nice powder blue. Grab 'em all, those will look great with the pinks and purples. Hey, let's put a few drifts of the yellow Achillea in there, too, to make the garden pop. There's a place behind the sea thrift where they'll fit, though I'm not sure if blooming times of those two will overlap – oh well! Come on, let's go, we're burning daylight!"

Now, granted, by the time I was city horticulturist, I had been working with plants for about 10 years, so I knew bloom times, heights, sizes, and the quirks of these plants. Pantsing is tougher when you don't have that information already in mind. For beginners, a design is a road map – and once you have your map, you can take little side tours. A map is a guide, not an edict.

In short, have fun with the process. If something doesn't work in your garden, you can always dig it up, or hide it under a birdbath, or grow vines over it.

Look for design ideas

Designing a garden is a lot of fun. This is where you get to meet all the possibilities that are open to you. But if you're new to this, coming up with design ideas can be tough. Sometimes that's true of the old gardening pro, too! Here are a few ways to get some good ideas (and these work if you're a seasoned gardener, too).

Go visit other gardens to see how plants look, and to see how different combinations work. Visit a botanical garden (though keep in mind that some of those plants might not be available to you – but you can certainly get some great ideas about form, color, and good design from these places.) Take pictures or notes of plant combinations you like as you come across them. When I see a landscape design I like, I make a sketch of it to see how it works, and figure out how I can replicate it at home or elsewhere. Don't be shy about writing down good plant choices or sketching garden layouts.

Some magazines, books, and websites have garden designs to look at. Look over the design, look at the pics, and if you see some plant combination you like, write it down or download the picture. Or pick up the landscape plan for yourself and modify it to your liking. By playing with different plant combinations, and seeing what works in the garden (and what doesn't), you can come up with ideas for your own garden.

Drawing the Design

Once you have all these measured out, sit down with your graph paper, let one square equal one square foot (adjust this if you have the graph paper with the tiny squares), and start putting this all down on paper. Have the top of the paper be north, and draw a little arrow pointing that way to look more official.

As you do, you will find that you'll need to keep running out to measure more things in the yard in order to make everything line up correctly. You've measured the house and driveway, for example, but wait, how many feet do you have between the driveway and the east corner of the house? So you measure that. Where exactly does the oak tree sit in relation to the fence and the house? Measure that. Then you notice that, on paper, the fence and the house are not lining up correctly. So you remeasure that and try to figure out where and how they line up. The oak tree seems to have inadvertently shrunk, though you'd measured it twice. Maybe it's time to take up drinking. Well, okay, but only in moderation.

Of course, that's the way the old timers did it. (P.S. I am not old.) These days, you can fix up a nice landscape plan on your phone using an app, or get a more elaborate program for your laptop that will do more than just move a tree symbol around until it's placed in the exact right spot.

As you draw your plan, generally a good rule of thumb is to arrange them by height – tall plants in back, short plants in front. Or, if you have an island bed (that is, a garden bed that's right out in the middle of the yard, not attached to any fence or structure), plant the tallest plants in the middle, and the shortest on the edges. But you can also blend several different varieties of plants that are the same size, the same way as you would blend several different flowers in a flower arrangement, for a good mix of colors and shapes. You also can be casual on regimenting sizes. A garden isn't a lineup of soldiers on dress parade, after all.

Match the plants to the amount of sun that's available. Set your shade plants near the trees, while the full sun plants will need to be right out in the sun.

You can be as formal or carefree as you like. You can arrange your flowers in a parterre – that is, a very formal setting with neat rows, tidy edged shrubs. Or you can have a natural garden, with plants arranged as if they were growing in the wild. Chances are, your garden will be someplace between these two extremes.

For best results, always plant the green side up.

Also, to make more of an impact, plant your perennials in drifts of 3, 5, or 7. These groups provide more of an impact than just planting one of every plant (unless you have a specimen plant that's as big as an elephant).

COMING UP WITH PLANT IDEAS

Keep bloom times straight by getting organized

One of the challenges to designing a garden with perennials can be bloom times. As you leaf through your gardening catalog, or scroll through online selections, you might want to set Sea Thrift (Armeria) and its pink flowers against a cloud of bright yellow chrysanthemums. A great combination – except sea thrift blooms in the early spring and mums bloom in the fall. It would be a great color combination – if only they bloomed at the same time!

Here's an idea that might help. As you scroll through plant pictures on your computer, you might save the pictures of plants that interest you. If you see a picture of a perennial you like, save it to a folder on your computer or phone, and be sure to name the file with the name of that particular plant. Then you'll have a record of the plant you like, plus some good quality photographs of their bloom colors, which you can mix and match on your computer desktop to see which combinations you like the best.

Then, put these pictures in different folders according to their bloom times – early spring, late spring, early summer, late summer, early fall, late fall. This method will help you find colors that work together AND bloom at the same time.

This folder method will also help you design a garden that provides interest through all four seasons – spring, summer, fall, and winter. If your spring folder is stuffed with pictures, while your fall folder is just about empty, start searching for fall plants so you'll have more than two plants blooming in your garden in fall.

(I don't want to leave out the pen-and-ink folks here, though. If you'd rather not fuss with a computer, then get four envelopes, one for each season. Cut out and label pictures of perennials that you like, then file them in the envelope that correlates with their bloom time. You can arrange these photos just the same as you do with the computer pictures – just take care not to have any strong breezes blowing through your room when you've got these pictures out.)

Something that also helps is to have a list of when each perennial blooms and how long the blooms last. Gardening catalogs and websites can give you a pretty good idea of when these bloom times take place, but regional differences in weather and climate will throw your bloom times off. Do your best when writing down your list of bloom times. Use this to choose perennials and arrange them according to bloom times and color. Then, once you do get them in the ground, start a new list for your own area.

When I was city horticulturist, I kept a running list, not only for perennials, but for everything – trees, wildflowers, you name it. Due to global warming (and yes, if you've spent any time outside you know that this is happening), the budbreak times have been moving. Right now the growing season starts about two or three weeks earlier than it did ten years ago, and goes about two weeks later in the fall. Also, you get this weird winter stuff going on. Global warming has also been hard on birds, throwing migratory patterns and nesting times into confusion.

Even when I was horticulturing 10 years ago, I knew the old bloom times were not the same as what I was seeing in the field at that time. So I wrote down bloom times, whether they were in my gardens or somebody else's gardens. I also wrote down things like when the barn swallows returned, when certain trees started blooming and for how long. I wrote down when I saw the first insect pests such as rose slugs (these are actually wasp larvae), tent caterpillars, and bagworms. "Oh darling, look, it's the first bagworm of spring!" And I did this for several years.

I didn't keep this list simply for the bloom times, though this was a very useful thing to know. I wanted to keep on my toes and be ready for every horticultural event before it came down the pike. Every January, I got a big desk calendar for the new year. I'd sit down there with my gardening notebook and start going through the calendar, writing in the dates of when I could expect bagworms, or the rose slugs, or the tent caterpillars – but I also wrote in some plant event that happened at the same time.

You've heard of gardening maxims such as "plant sweet corn when the oak leaves are the size of a squirrel's ear" or "spray for bagworms when the catalpa trees bloom." These are events that you can time these events to – or could. But now the oak leaves are the size of a squirrel's ear in mid-April. The timing between the catalpa trees and the bagworms has fallen out of synch – because I'd look for bagworms when the catalpas were in bloom and the bagworms were already pretty big by that time.

These days, with the world's weather in flux, you have to figure out the new times for all gardening events. This isn't your grandma's gardening world anymore, folks, as much as I hate to say it. I wish it were. Those winters in the 1970s were a doozy, and we could build snow houses and go sled riding all the time. My son is five years old and has been sled riding once. Only once. What kind of childhood are we giving our children!

At any rate, have a place in your notebook for the "What's Blooming Now" list (adding in "What's Happening in the Natural World?" along with blooming times).

CREATING A FOUR-SEASON PERENNIAL GARDEN

You can design a garden that provides interest through all four seasons – spring, summer, fall, and winter. This is where you can really bring all elements of a plant into play – leaf color, form, shape – not just the blossoms.

In spring, summer, and fall, perennials will give you blossoms. The problem is that these blossoms last for a week, maybe a month at the most, before the plant is done blooming. (However, if you cut the perennials back when they are finished blooming, they might reward you with a second rush of blooms.)

One would do well to mix hot-season and cool-season plants in the garden, to make a longer-lasting show of color, instead of watching all the plants turn black at once when frost hits.

A garden for all seasons ... we'd start with some of the earliest-season bulbs, such as snowdrops and crocuses, coming up along the garden border. Then as the season progresses, other bulbs start blooming. With tulips and daffodils, you have early, mid-season, and late bloomers, so you could always have something blooming from March to May – though keep in mind that you'll also have the early-spring perennials blooming and hostas growing gracefully out of the ground.

Then in fall, you also have the option of using cool-season annuals, fall-blooming perennials, and bulbs such as fall crocuses to extend the season. Then, for winter interest, you could have ornamental grasses and the dried flowers of honesty, or money plant; you could have red-twigged dogwood; you could have a Harry Lauders walking stick (*Corylus avellana* "Contorta") with its corkscrew branches. Or grow a witch hazel tree for its yellow blooms in February, or holly with its red berries.

Variegated leaves add color to perennial gardens

To keep the garden colorful, grow perennials with colorful leaves. There's been a big push over the last decade or more to breed plants with variegated leaves, as well as purple, maroon, or chartreuse leaves. Coral bells (Heuchera) were a cute edging plant in the early 1990s, but since then, breeders have been having a field day with this plant, creating a dazzling array of colors in the leaves alone. In one garden catalog, I can find Heuchera in lime, white, maroon, flame-red, deep orange, chartreuse, bright red, rich caramel, deep burgundy, amber, yellow and pink, purple, and silver. And this rainbow doesn't even include the tiny bell-like flowers, which bloom in bright red, pink, yellow, and white in early summer (though on some plants, the flowers' colors clash with their own leaves). Heucheras were traditionally a shade plant, but the new varieties seem to take more sun than their predecessors.

For a softer, shimmering look, you can plant silver-leaved plants such as Lambs Ears (*Stachys byzantina*). The Lamb's Ears has soft gray leaves that are shaped like lambs ears and are actually fun to pet. Little kids (and grownups) love to pat the leaves. Their flowers are pink, on soft gray stalks, but some people cut down the flowers to keep the soft gray leaves looking pretty.

Artemesia is another gray plant that comes in many different shapes and sizes. You can get Silver Mound (*Artemesia schmidtiana*), which is a soft gray low-growing plant, also a nice plant for little kids (and grownups!) to pat. Or Artemesia 'Powis Castle,' a gray leaved plant that is much taller.

Sedums, a kind of succulent that thrives even when it's dryer than heck outside, and recent years have also seen an amazing proliferation of these plants in the nursery industry. With the sedum, you get more subtle leaf colors than with the Heuchera, but they are still stunning. Many of the sedums are low-growing plants with thick, water-filled leaves, and so these plants can really take care of themselves. They also come in a variety of sizes, shapes and leaf forms. Some plants seem to bristle, though they are thornless, while other plants have soft, rounded leaves. Sedum leaves can be found in shades of silver, deep red, chartreuse, burgundy, while the blossoms (these by the way are lovely) are in all shades and sizes.

Sedum 'Autumn Joy' is a very hardy perennial that bloom in the fall and are visited by monarchs, skipper butterflies, wasps, and bees, and many other insects. It's a lot of fun to watch the diversity of insects and butterflies that visit this plant.

Ornamental grasses can also add color and off-season interest. So even if you have a gap between blooming times in your garden, you can fill the color gap with foliage.

Add shrubs and trees to extend the garden's color through fall and winter

Perennials with colorful leaves give you many options for creating a garden that looks great all year around, even if the flowers you've carefully chosen turn out to have a lull in flowering for a week or two. Of course, you can mix some annuals and shrubs into your garden if you like to add more color and winter interest.

When building a garden, many folks prefer to plant a mixed border – that is, a garden strip that mixes shrubs, perennials, and annuals. This is a solid idea, because shrubs provide four-season interest (in winter, they might have red berries, interesting bark, or red-colored twigs), or can be grown as an eye-catching specimen that the border is structured around. Annuals provide a big splash of constant color from spring until frost kills them off, and perennials offer their own colors and interest during their blooming times. These different kinds of plants providing interest in the border in their own special ways – and it shows the value of diversity.

For instance, a small witch hazel tree will give you blooms in February. Other trees, such as paperbark maple (*Acer griseum*) have papery bark with grays and orangeish reds that add winter interest. Red Twig Dogwoods (*Cornus alba* 'Sibirica'), a shrub with brilliant red twigs, adds interest all winter long, and in late spring has little yellow flowers followed by small blue berries.

For fall, you have fall flowers but also fall color, if you mix in shrubs like burning bush, which turns bright red in the fall, or fothergilla, which turns a lovely shade of yellow. You can also plant stuff with berries on it, or shrubs with red twigs or neat bark for winter interest, and grasses for architectural possibilities. Sea holly (*Eryngium*), a lovely but prickly perennial, has an amazing shape, very formal and Roman, for the garden.

Now, what looks great to one gardener might not work for another. Some gardeners leave ornamental grasses standing in the winter because they like their shape in the landscape. Other gardeners cut them down as soon as they die off in late fall. Some people like to plant hostas all around the trunks of their trees, both for foliage color and to keep the weeds down around the tree. Some people are bored by hostas and prefer only mulch around their trees. At any rate, it's a free country (or it was at press time, anyway).

When you're choosing perennials, also choose plants that offer different kinds of interest besides blooms. Add architecturally interesting plants, those of different shapes, forms, and textures. I always think of sea holly, which is a type of thistle, but it has a stunningly formal shape in the garden, as if it should be on a coat of arms. I have seen these in person, and they are very interesting to look at (though, being a thistle, it is also very prickly). I always want to pair it with pastels – but it would be a good idea to wear rose gauntlets when working with these.

So, also consider mixing up different forms and seeing what this does to the overall effect.

ADD FRAGRANCE TO THE PERENNIAL BORDER

Fragrance is an aspect of the perennial garden that is often overlooked – but it adds so much good that it needs to be included every single time.

Good fragrant perennials include *Dianthus*, or pinks, which keep coming back and can withstand any weather, it seems. Pinks are related to carnations, except they are hardier, tougher, and a lovely addition to the front of your garden. A favorite pink is the Cheddar Pink, *Dianthus gratianapolitanus*. Say that real fast three times. Or not. The cheddar pinks bear magenta-pink flowers with a clove-like fragrance, and the bluish-gray foliage makes a good ground cover or rock garden plant. Any other dianthus are good choices for the perennial border. These are tough little plants and cute as bugs. When they get done blooming, shear off all the spent blossoms to clean up the plant and also to get some fall flowers as well.

I've always loved lavender plants, though they aren't always reliable in zone 5, where I am. Back in the day, when I walked my dog in my old neighborhood, I sometimes passed by a house that had this lovely, 20 foot border full of lavender plants. They were enormous for Missouri, and were gorgeous and fragrant, and I liked to pick a little sprig to carry with me as my bulldog muscled his way down the sidewalk. But one spring when I walked by, I was dismayed to see them all gone except for one. Though that particular winter didn't seem bad to me, apparently the lavenders all though it was, and nearly all of them had succumbed to the weather.

Lavender plants will need winter protection up north. Never cut them back before May, as they often start growing late. Plant them in a "sweet" soil; that is, one to which lime has been added. They don't like acidic soil at all.

Phlox is a fragrant favorite, though I haven't had the best luck with these in our humid Midwest climate. *Phlox paniculata* tends to catch powdery mildew here, just as lilacs do. However, our native phlox, Phlox divericata, does just fine here in a shade garden. This phlox bears pastel purple blossoms in May and June and smells sweet. And these days, many varieties of phlox have been bred to be mildew-resistant. Their spicy vanilla-clove fragrance is a sweet addition to any garden.

DWARF OR NANA COMPACTA PHLOX.

Irises have long been a favorite. The popular perennial, the Japanese iris, is a great low-maintenance plant but is unscented. These day, you can buy an incredible array of irises of every color imaginable, and they all smell so good.

Clematis are usually not fragrant, though the Sweet Autumn clematis (*Clematis terniflora*—sometimes mislabeled as *Clematis paniculata*, formerly *Clematis maximowitcziana* – help help I can't keep up!) blooms in fall and has a powerful fragrance. It can be invasive, so keep an eye on it as it will spread and reseed. However, it's a very easy plant to grow (obviously) and doesn't need a lot of care, and will turn into a thick vine covered with small white flowers in fall. I let one take over the fence in the chicken yard so the girls (and boy) can have a cool little oasis out of the sun during the day. Once the plant is done blooming and winter's coming on, I can cut the whole thing down. In fact, this year I cut it down to the ground in early spring and it simply sprang back from the roots and is well on its way to arbor size as it was last year.

Don't plant this clematis in the south, however, as it is very invasive. In Virginia, for instance, it will take over woodland areas like you wouldn't believe.

Clematis montana 'Mayleen' is also a fragrant clematis, though not as insanely tough (or invasive) as the previous plant – but this is easier to keep in bounds. It bears pink, four-petaled blossoms with a light fragrance. However, these are not as cold-hardy as the sweet autumn clematis, hardy only in zones 6 through 9. So northerners might be out of luck, unfortunately.

Oriental lilies are lovely and fragrant. (How do you tell them apart from Asiatic lilies? Asiatic lilies have no scent, they sport smooth, glossy petals, and they bloom in bright colors of orange, dark pink, and yellow. Oriental lilies are super-fragrant, are usually larger than the Asiatic lilies, generally bloom in soft shades of white, red and pink, and their petals are not smooth but slightly shaggy.) Also *Viola* 'Columbine' and 'Rebecca' have a nice scent.

In annuals, Heliotrope is always a winner, as well as Stock and Mignonette. Scented Geraniums come in many different aromas, leaf shapes, and blossoms.

The sense of smell is so neglected. Live in a world of fragrance for a while.

WHAT TO LOOK FOR IN CONTAINER-GROWN PLANTS

In spring, when the nurseries open, it's easy to forget what you're doing and just start grabbing trees and other plants with nary a thought to what you're grabbing. However, when you're shopping, there are certain things you need to watch for ... and watch out for.

If overall the plants look sad, underwatered, or the foliage looks odd, go to a different place. Many retail stores, though the plants they sell are cheap, are really bad about taking care of plants, leaving them to wilt, or overwatering them, or trying to sell plants with whiteflies all over them. It is true that you get what you pay for! Check the retail stores for bargains, but if you want a good-quality plant, you might have to start at your local nurseries.

Perennials and annuals

Look for healthy plants with no bugs, and healthy-colored leaves (leaves that are really pale, or have a strange-looking pale veins that other leaves don't, are suspect).

If the plants seem perpetually wilted, or overwatered, don't buy them.

Look for plants that are robust with deep green foliage (unless the foliage is supposed to be a different color, of course), lots of strong stems, and leaves that are clean of defects and funny brown spots.

It's better to buy a plant that's not blooming. If the plant has blossoms, it's a good idea to take off the flowers before you plant it. Plants tend to direct all their energy toward blossoms, so they wouldn't be working so hard on important things -- like growing roots!

Fall is a great time to buy and plant perennials

Fall is the second spring, in a sense, where you can get back out into the yard to sow grass seed and plant perennials and shrubs and trees. Also, now that the heat's broken, the plants come out of their summer-imposed dormancy and concentrate on growing once more. During drought and intense heat, plants divert their energy toward conserving water, which means they cut back on blooming or growing. That's why the roses all start blooming their heads off. And who can blame them.

A newly planted perennial in summer heat will curl up and wilt. This is because the summer heat is evaporating the water out of the plant faster than the roots can supply water to the leaves. Planting in the cool of fall, when the evaporation rate isn't as high, will keep the plant from going dry and wilting, and the plant can use its energy to send roots deep.

GARDEN BED INSTALLATION

At last, the big day. Go out there with a garden hose and weed killer. Lay the garden hose where you want the edge of the bed, and then play with the look of the garden.

When you are actually out there figuring out how big you want your garden bed, you have choices. You can go for a straight line edge, which is easier to maintain, though a little boring. Or you can try a curving garden's edge, which gives a garden a more natural look, but is a little more tricky to mow around. I prefer curved edges, if I can, as I'm not a very precise mower anyway.

So take your garden hose and outline where you want your garden bed. Try a straight edge, then experiment with a curved edge, or an edge that gently flows with the natural contours of the land. Try different looks and see which works best for you.

For best results, turn on your mower (obviously, leave the blades off so you don't tear up your garden hose) and run it along the edge of where you want your garden bed to be. See if mowing is easy or tricky. Then you can make adjustments before you start digging.

Once you've settled on an area and edge that is right for you – not too big – spray weed killer on the grass/weeds there (if you are carving a garden bed out of your lawn) and let it do its work for a day or two.

If you need the garden hose for something else during that time, mark the edge of the garden with lime, flour, or landscape paint.

Then get an edger, a flat shovel and a regular shovel, and maybe a tiller if you need to break up the soil, if you've never had a garden there before. The grass will probably have to come out for best results. Now, if you're putting in a garden bed in a location prone to erosion, like the side of a hill, take a little longer making sure the grass has been killed of – then use a weed-whacker to scalp off the grass, and install the bed leaving some of the grass roots in to help hold the soil in place.

In most other instances, though, the work goes more smoothly if you till up the dead grass, or slice it off the top of the ground with a good, sharp spade. Grass roots tend to get tangled up in tillers, which is a hassle.

HOW TO REVAMP YOUR PERENNIAL BED

It rains. Then it's clear for a few days, and you wait and wait to do a little garden work. When the ground is just dry enough, you head out there with your shovel, whistling the theme from "A Fistful of Dollars" (We can fight!).

Just as you set the shovel in, even as you brace your foot on the shovel to break the ground, the sky breaks open and dumps 55 gallons of water over your head and on your garden, making it impossible to dig. "Heh heh," say the clouds, then they drift away to play the same joke on someone else.

That about describes the last several weeks. Still, I was able to get out recently and get all the perennials moved around in my garden (the 20-foot one). I walked like the Hunchback of Notre Dame for a week after, but I'm glad to be finished with that.

I'd meant to get the perennials all moved around last year, but for some reason or another, I never did it. So, the moving was a little like cleaning out Fibber McGee's closet: Don't open that door!

At one point I had at least 10 plants out of the ground, languishing in the shade of the old lilac (which needs to be rejuvenated badly) as I tried to get enough ground clear and raked level so I could put them back in.

What was neat was that I found several plants that I had believed dead. Two lilies that didn't come up last year were peeking through the soil under some asters, and the same asters were hiding a sedum a friend had given me. And, in a shovelful of soil I was carting out of the way, I found a little delphinium that I thought had succumbed to bacterial spot.

The whole operation went pretty well, and the impromptu design does have some coherence. It looks pretty good until you get to the far right of the garden, the last bit of garden I did.

One of the big rules in garden design is: Buy either three or five of one plant, so you have a drift of color that can be seen.

I disregarded the rule a few times, buying plants that I meant to try them out and then get some more (and never did). So most of the garden's design looks pretty coherent, because I have huge drifts of yarrow and asters (very huge) and Russian sage. But suddenly at the far right of the garden, there's one Shasta daisy, one gallardia, one daylily, etc. It's a mess!

But there's an island bed I need to finish, after I reseed the lawn ...

SOILBUILDING

I can't bear to stay in the greenhouse when it's so nice and sunny outside. I do like to walk through, looking at all the bright green geraniums. (It must be the seaweed extract I sprayed them with last week.) But I gotta keep walking, there's a lot to do. Who knows what the weather's going to do tomorrow?

I'm going to dig a pile of soil out of the garden at Felix Street Square. That awful clay is among the worst soil I've ever seen. It has got to go! So it will.

That digging is the fun part.

(It's not really fun.)

But it does turn out good when you consider the end result – beautiful soil, happy plants ... my gosh, I could actually have a decent garden here. So I dig, slicing into the clay, bending the knees to heft the soil into the truck bed, then set the shove into the soil again, about nine inches deep.

Once in a while I have to lean on my shovel and catch my breath, muscles aching. Wow. How can I move all this dirt?

But it's satisfying, seeing it go. I can see the work I'm accomplishing. Sometimes, when I work on a story (or this column,) it's hard to keep going because I don't ever feel like I'm getting anywhere – I'm just floundering in words and making a mess. But when I dig a big hole in the ground, I can see the results (though if I'm not careful, I can fall in it).

At the day's end, I dump the compost in and rake it out. It is a rich, dark brown. The part of the garden I haven't been able to finish digging up is a pasty yellow color. When I get all this soil replaced, I'm going to be a happy lady.

I'm also going to be built like Arnold Schwarzenegger.

Aerate, add good things to improve your soil

"How do you improve your soil without all that digging?" my Grandma Ann asked.

That's a good question. I've been pondering it myself, because I am sick and tired of digging. I've dug out enough clay hardpan and shoveled enough compost for this year, thank you very much!

Soil is fascinating (when you're not digging in it). The soil's ecosystem is teeming with worms, ants, bacteria (many of which are good – even the bacteria on your hands), protozoa, springtails, miles and miles of fungi, moles and voles – the list goes on and on. All of these creatures enrich the soil in one way or another.

Worms are a good indicator of how alive your soil is. If you don't see many worms when you dig, your soil may need help.

Some sources actually say that it's best not to dig too much, because excessive digging and tilling can tear apart the ecosystems that already exist in the soil. I can get behind that theory.

So, how do you improve the soil?

First, get a soil test from the University Extension Center to find out what the soil needs – or doesn't need. They have information about how to take a soil test and how to read the results.

Next, use a pitchfork, or put on a pair of cleats, and punch holes in the ground for aeration.

Then add the good stuff. An inch-thick layer of compost or well-rotted manure works wonders, releasing nutrients over the long term. Use bone meal to add phosphorus or blood meal to add nitrogen.

Enviro-Max, a product being sold at local nurseries, helps open pores in the soil that allow the soil to breathe. You spray it on the ground, then water it in deeply.

Finally, compost tea feeds your soil ecosystem and increases fertility. Put some compost in an old sock, tie off the end, and soak it in a bucket of rainwater for several days. Pour that on the garden and then step back. Your plants will love it.

PERENNIAL CARE

When The Growing Gets Tough
The Tough Get Growing

There's a cute little dayflower growing in the back of my truck, out of the sandbag that I haven't cleared out from last winter.

Actually, the dayflower isn't so cute, since it's wilting from heat and lack of water. But it's hanging in there. When it rains, it revives and gives us cerulean-blue flowers.

Occasionally, social conscience whispers, "What will the neighbors think? Pull it up!" But I can't do it. You've got to respect something that survives despite such oppressive odds. Besides, anything that tough would probably fight its eviction, even bite.

I've seen dayflowers hybridized for larger flowers being sold as annuals under their scientific name, *Commelina*. Would that be a sure bet for a garden that doesn't get much care? You bet. They're also related to a plant that's native to Missouri called *Tradescantia*. A good choice for Midwestern gardens? Heck yes.

Last winter I read an article by a British garden writer (but who among the garden writers isn't British) who said that every time she left the garden for a time, the wimpy plants died but the tough plants survived. She said that if she left the garden alone often enough, after a while it wouldn't need her anymore.

That's my garden, filled with plants that can take a licking and keep on, er, growing, come drought, floods, inquisitive dogs, lawnmowers, etc.

Native plants always are the best bet. They have put up with Missouri conditions for ages, so whatever the weather unleashes will be old news to them. Heck, any plants that have been run over by buffalo herds time and time again are exceptionally good candidates.

Lately we've been seeing a lot of these prairie plants, such as black-eyed Susan (or *Rudbeckia*), as well as the popular coneflower, which is the *Echinacea* of pharmaceutical fame.

Buzz through a copy of Missouri Wildflowers (available from the Missouri Department of Conservation) to meet tough plants like joe-pye weed, queen-of-the-prairie, perennial geraniums, spiderwort, and pinks. Many of these can be bought through catalogs or local nurseries.

When you plant them, don't coddle them or water the heck out of them. This goes for tulips, too. Did you know that, in their native habitat, they face hot, dry summers? So if you heavily water and fertilize the annuals the tulips grow under, they won't do well next year. Replicate the plant's original habitat, and the plant is happy.

FERTILIZING THE PERENNIAL GARDEN (OR, FEED 'EM AND REAP)

Unlike roses, which chug Miracle-Gro as if it were water, perennials don't need a whole lot of extra fertilizer. In fact, if you give them too much fertilizer, perennials get leggy and tend to flop. Or, your perennials become particularly juicy from too much nitrogen in their fertilizer, they get attacked by various diseases and insects. Or, the perennials might end up being more interested in producing leaves than blossoms.

Now, a moderate amount of fertilizer is perfectly fine. A good time to throw down granular fertilizer is in early spring, when the new growth is pushing up. And it's also fine to give the perennials some Miracle-Gro in late spring as they get all geared up for summer. A slow-release fertilizer, broadcast around the plants, should last for three to six months, depending on brand and quality.

Now, some perennials will need a little more fertilizing. Daylilies, peonies, chrysanthemums, and phlox like a spring and a summer feeding. Also, delphiniums, daisies, and lungwort (Pulmonaria) will be happy to get a little Miracle-Gro in mid-season.

But the very best thing that you can do for your perennials (and your soil) is to add compost.

I used to wonder what the big deal about compost was. I'd look at the numbers on a bag of compost. Usually they're something super-low, like 1-3-1. (These numbers show the amount of the three main elements that the bag of compost has – that is, 1% Nitrogen, 3% Phosphorus, 1% Potassium. NPK, if you use the chemical symbols.) The amount of NPK in, say Miracle-Gro, is usually something like 30-30-30. That's a lot! And yet many plant people urge you to use compost on the soil. Why is that?

It's because compost is full of humus, which builds the soil like no man-made fertilizer can do.

Soil works best when it's a living organism. That sounds like weird stuff, but hear me out. The best soil, whether it's sandy, silty, clay, or loam, always consists of several things. It contains a good amount of organic material. The organic material provides food for the organisms that live in the soil – an untold number of arthropods (insects and other critters), bacteria, protozoa, worms, nematodes, etc etc. When you have a flourishing ecosystem underground, they make the area great for plant roots. Some of these creatures help break down organic materials into bits small enough for plant roots to absorb. Some soil organisms, actually increases the reach of plant roots so they can pull more nutrients and chemicals and elements out of the soil, which makes them healthier.

Organic material is the bedrock, so to speak, of good soil function. But if you don't replenish the organic material in the soil, eventually, the creatures of the soil cannot find any more to eat. They die, becoming organic material themselves.

But in each generaltion that dies off, they leave less and less of themselves in the soil, until they're gone for good. And without organic material and busy soil organisms to keep the soil alive, the soil becomes this pallid, dusty place. The soil also becomes very hard to work, hard to break, and when you do break it up, it has no cohesion. Plants will grow in this soil, but they won't thrive.

Leafmold – that is, decaying or chopped-up leaves – is also a very good soil amendment. If you have a mulching mower, empty a bunch of bags of leaves out and run the mower over them again and again until they're chopped up. Use this as a mulch on your perennials. If you're worried about the leaves blowing around, then cover the leaves with a mulch of wood chips. The leafmold will slowly decay under the wood chips, adding many good things to your soil.

Leaves are an excellent source of nutrients. Tree roots reach deep into the soil and bring up elements that have been locked away from the surface for eons. Many of these elements end up in the leaves, which fall to the ground and become fertilizer in forests and, unfortunately, landfill fodder in lawns. Use those leaves in your garden instead of sending them to the landfill.

Here's the kicker: If you add one inch of compost or leafmold to your garden every year, you don't even need to fertilize. The University Extension service says so. How about that for a low-cost solution?

FREE PLANTS!
DIVIDE YOUR PERENNIALS

I enjoy perennials for a number of reasons. You don't cripple your hands and wrists from planting millions of them every spring. In May, while annuals are still small and wimpy, perennials are already massive. Some perennials, such as candytuft, flax, irises, saxifrage, and columbines, are blooming before it's even warm enough to put annuals in the ground. Finally, when you need more perennials, all you have to do is divide the ones that are already in your garden.

Dividing perennials is generally more traumatic to the gardener than it is to the plant itself. Plants thrive after they've been divided – and you get all these free plants in the bargain. Also, undivided perennials stop blooming; once divided, they will start flowering again. You can't lose!

Perennials can be divided all fall, even into the winter. You should, however, try to get them divided several weeks before the ground freezes so the roots can get settled in before the real cold begins. The nice thing about dividing the plants in the fall is that they have all winter, and all next spring, to get established before the awful heat of summer hits. In fact, most plants are quietly, slowly growing their roots even during the cold of winter. So while there seems to be nothing growing on the surface, there's still plenty going on underground. Plants are neat.

So, when should you divide a perennial? Well, if they have a large dead spot in the middle of the plant; if the plant has stopped blooming in the last few years; if the plant flops over when it used to stand up just fine; or if the plant looks crowded. Some perennials need dividing every few years, while some prefer less often.

Some shouldn't be divided at all, such as gas plant (*Dictamnus alba*), indigo (*Baptisia*), baby's breath, and columbines. Plants that are actually small woody shrubs shouldn't be divided either. These include candytuft (*Iberis sempervirens*), lavender, santolina, and artemesia.

Before dividing a plant, there are several things you should do. If the soil is dry, water the plants deeply a few days before you do the job. Dry soil will break apart, tearing the roots. By the same rule, see that the soil is not too wet, because digging while it is muddy will ruin the soil structure.

Prepare the place where you're going to plant the divisions by digging some good, deep holes. Add bone meal, compost, or other good organic fertilizers to the soil and mix them in, loosening up the soil around the planting area as you do. Pull or dig up any weeds in the area, too. Give the plant the best soil you possibly can. Your plants will love you for it.

Protip: Always have the holes dug and ready to go *before* you start moving the perennials. This way, your perennials aren't just lying in the sun with their roots drying up while you dig the holes – instead, you can dig them up and then stick them right back in the ground.

Now the fun part. go to the perennials, shovel in hand. Clean up any dead leaves and stems around the plants. If the perennial is really big and tall, cut it back to a reasonable height.

I've found that the most effective method of dividing a plant is to dig up the perennial's entire rootball. Then – and this is important – *put the plant back in the hole.* Make the dividing cuts by slicing into the plant with the shovel. If the plant is very tough and rootbound, I will jump onto the shovel to make the cuts. Then lever the separated plants out for transplanting.

I do this because rootballs tend to roll away when you attack them with a shovel. Also, when the plant's sitting in the ground, you can see the natural parts (as in the place where you *part* your hair) in the plant, and there's where you make the cuts. Sometimes this involves some fancy work with the shovel. Finally, the divisions stay cool and moist in the ground until you move them, instead of drying out in the sun.

Another way of dividing perennials is to pull the perennial out of the ground, then stick two garden forks into the middle of the plant you're dividing. The forks should have their backs to each other and be close together. Then you use the forks to pry the plants apart. Once the crowns are separated, you can use a knife or some clippers to cut the roots apart.

If you want a lot of new plants and you don't care how  small they are, you can shake off as much soil as you can and then just take the plant apart, making judicious cuts with the clippers. Daylilies, if not too overgrown, can be taken apart this way. You end up getting a half million tiny plants that won't look like much for a year. Plant them in

Hemerocallis fulva (Kwanso) fl. pl.

some hidden spot in the garden until they get big enough to show off.

Some plants, like indigo (Baptisia), have very tough, woody crowns that you'll have to take a knife to. Chop it in half, or quarters, making sure each section has at least one or two eyes and roots. (Like I say, the Baptisia do not like being divided or transplanted, so take care when you're doing this.)

Overcrowded irises might come out of the ground as one big plate. You can cut or break them apart; they don't mind. Replant them shallowly, with the top of the rhizome sticking a little out of the soil. You end up with bags and bags of leftover rhizomes from this operation.

Peonies and other tuberous plants will need to be dug up and dunked in a bucket of water so you can find the buds on the tuber. Cut the tuber apart so each section will have several buds and roots, then plant. Peonies might not bloom the next year, but at least they'll get some good growing done.

Once you've divided them, discard any diseased or really wimpy-looking plants. Also discard the old centers, or crowns, of the plant.

If you do need to leave the new divisions out for a while, keep them shaded and protected from the wind until you can get them planted. If it's going to be several days, you might just dump them back in their old hole, cover them with mulch, and water them.

Plant the divisions in their new locations – please be sure to give each plenty of room to grow – and water them in well. Around the base of the plants, place a layer of newspapers, about five pages deep. Then pile about two or three inches of mulch over that. (Of course, if the plant is small, put down less mulch.) The newspaper will stop weed seeds before they can germinate, and keep the roots protected from the winter cold and from next summer's sun, and the mulch will make the area look nice and tidy. Give them a good drink every week, if you don't get an inch of rain, until it freezes. You might give the perennials a quart or two of water on temperate days through the winter if the season has been dry. Then you're set. Enjoy!

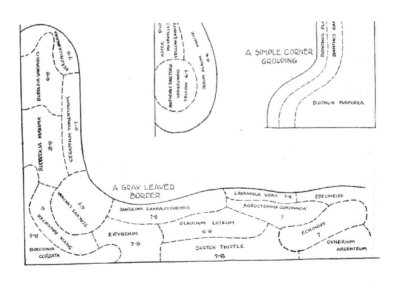

WHAT PLANT TAGS ACTUALLY MEAN

Plant tags make all kinds of crazy claims. But do you know what the truth is? The problem with plant tags is that the people who write them up are not allowed to tell the unvarnished truth about the plant, even if the plant is a real dog. If they do speak, highly suspicious things happen to them. I was able to wrest a few secrets out of one such writer before she met her doom in a freak rose accident. Here's a primer on what the plant tag says ... and what it actually means.

Reseeds freely – And will replace your entire lawn with tiny, wicked clones

Fast-growing vine – Plant it ... and run

May be invasive – Resistance is futile. You will be assimilated

Easy to care for – Will require care!

Low-maintenance – Will require maintenance!

Fragrant flowers – Even as the rest of the plant defoliates freely due to blackspot/small hungry bugs/evil imps

Size varies – From the size of a breadbox to the size of your house.

Vigorous – To the detriment of every plant around it

Many uses for this plant – None of which you have ever heard of

Semi-dwarf – About a few inches shorter than normal

Disease-free rose – Ha ha ha ha ha!

Fashionable – For the next five minutes, after which it will become an embarrassment

Old-fashioned – With all the ill-mannered traits that made plant breeders scramble to hybridize it

Godetia (Satin Rose).

Satin Rose—Very large showy annual. Rich velvety **satin rose. Pkt. 3c.**

GILIA TRICOLOR

A very showy annual that blooms easy and always. Pkt. 3c.

[Fig. 12.]

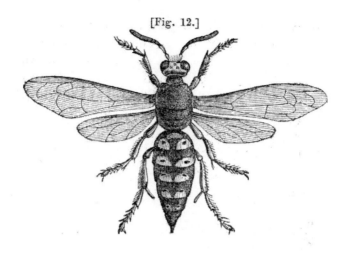

WASPS: GREAT PREDATORS FOR YOUR PERENNIAL GARDEN

Yes, yes, I know what people think about wasps. When I was a kid, they'd get into the house and fly around and I would be the first to grab the scissors and cut them into twitching bits. I was so morbid. But now all that has changed. I like wasps!

I grew to like wasps when I was in college. I had my writing desk set against a window with wasp's nest in it, and since I never got around to taking the nest down, I ended up getting a close-up view of how wasps live, and began to enjoy watching them after a while.

The part I liked best was feeding time, when one of the wasps would squeeze in under the outside pane. She had in her mouth (i.e. mandibles) a round ball of some greenish stuff, which I discovered later were chewed-up caterpillars. When she gained her feet, she buzzed drunkenly up to the nest, then would spend some time turning the ball of green meat in her front legs, chewing and softening it all the while, before tearing off pieces and feeding them to the grubs. When mealtime was over, she always washed herself carefully, like a cat.

Most people are not too crazy about wasps, and with good reason. Last week, Park and Rec workers took out a wasp's nest at Krug Park after wasps stung a girl twice. But if the nest is out of the way, wasps are beneficial to your garden.

Wasps catch the bugs that wreak havoc with your plants. Wasps feed a lot of bug meat to their larvae – which is from those aphids and caterpillars that were eating your plants. Wasps also help pollinate flowers.

Different varieties of wasps go after different kinds of bugs. For example, mud daubers will capture small spiders for its young, and cicada killers, which are very large wasps, eat cicadas.

There's a cicada killer that hangs around the rose garden, pouncing on little pieces of mulch that (I guess) she keeps mistaking for cicadas. She apparently needs a pair of glasses. She's a big, mean-looking wasp, almost two inches long with black and yellow stripes. But I've nearly stepped on her several times but she's never made any threatening moves. She ignores me when I walk through her territory. I'm tempted to bring her a cicada, just so she stops trying to kill mulch.

Robert Frost, the Vermont poet, allowed white-faced hornets into his kitchen because they were so good at catching flies. Once in a while, though, the hornets would go after things that looked like flied, including huckleberries.

"He stooped and struck a little huckleberry the way a player curls around a football .... The huckleberry rolled him on his head," Frost wrote in "The White-Faced Hornet."

Other varieties of wasps are beneficial because they lay their eggs in living caterpillars or other insects. The eggs hatch and the larvae devour the poor caterpillar from within.

Sometimes, a wasp's nest is too close for comfort, such as when they build one in your garden hose caddy. If you have to kill wasps, find a spray that allows you to stand far way when you're spraying it, and keep your eyes open for wasps defending their home. Always be ready to run!

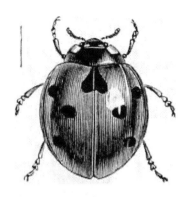

LADYBUGS – A GREAT FAVORITE IN THE GARDEN

Several years ago, I read about a gardener who bought a box of ladybugs a little too early in the year and accidentally let them loose in her house.

For weeks she walked on tiptoes, afraid to crush the ladybugs -- but her houseplants were free of pests. Finally, when spring came around, she was able to open her windows and doors and shoo the ladybugs out. Then her outside plants were free of pests as well.

This is why ladybugs are one of the most popular bugs in gardening: They are definitely bug eaters. I've picked up Asian ladybugs – the large ladybugs that congregate on the sides of houses in the fall – and they start chewing on the skin in the palm of my hands. They don't bite, they just start scraping, and it tickles. It's one of those strange ladybug things, I guess. One of my coworkers kept getting bitten by these Asian ladybugs. "Why do they keep biting me?" he asked me.

"You must have done something to make them mad," I told him.

We shared the "house full of ladybugs" mentality of the aforementioned garden writer late this spring at the city's greenhouse, when we began finding ladybugs outside and started bringing them in to see how well they would control pests. The aphids and whiteflies we were trying to control were not bothered by the sprays I was using

It's too bad we didn't find those ladybugs earlier. I would have loved to have a few helping me over the winter.

Linda Zoubek, intrepid greenhouse volunteer, used a paintbrush to collect the ladybug larvae, which were as tiny as the small letters on this page. She then would rush them to the greenhouse and release them on the aphid-ridden cosmos.

Once she found the ladybugs and larvae and brought them in, they multiplied fast. And those guys also grew. Pretty soon, ladybug larvae of various shapes and sizes were running around on the cosmos, and they could move fast.

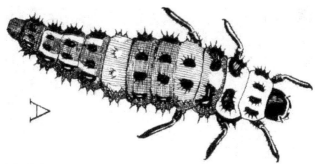

A ladybug larva (larger than actual size, obviously)

Ladybug larvae are voracious eaters and are shaped like tiny lizards, or Komodo dragons. They are black with two little orange spots toward their head and have a long tail. They start out small, but eventually, through successive molts, they get bigger. Some of the larvae in the greenhouse were about a centimeter long when they went through their final metamorphosis into ladybug form. (Ladybugs, being members of the beetle family, will go through a full metamorphosis: egg, larva, pupa, adult. This part is the pupa stage, similar to the cocoon stage in the butterfly family.)

When they would metamorphose, the larvae would attach themselves to the cosmos stem by their tail and would curl into an upside-down comma. They would seem to bloat a little. Soon, the lower half of them would turn orange, then the upper half.

After about a week or two, the old skin would break down the back and the new ladybug would push itself out. After a short stay, the ladybugs tended to fly away, but some of the ladybugs laid eggs before they left, and pretty soon there were more tiny larvae creeping around.

I enjoyed raising ladybugs and watching them (and their larvae) eat the aphids. As far as we could tell, they preferred aphids but didn't bother with whiteflies. That's a shame, but I hear that you can buy tiny wasps to attack them. Hmm! The tiny larvae are still around; apparently, ladybugs lay eggs through the year. My Grandma and I found one late in the year, crawling around on her impatiens. I say, more power to it. We need all the help we can get.

GET RID OF APHIDS BY GETTING RID OF ANTS

Aphids are small bugs, but they can overwhelm your plants fast because they reproduce. Not only do aphids lay eggs at an alarming rate, but they can also give live birth without mating! Yet the tiny pear-shaped bugs have no exoskeleton to protect them from predators. Any ladybug or lacewing can find them and eat them up.

So how do aphids survive so successfully?

The answer: Ants protect them. Ants keep aphids in herds, like cows, "milking" them for their honeydew. When an ant strokes an aphid's back with its antennae, the aphid will secrete a drop of honeydew – sugar water. Naturally, the ants love this, so they're quick to protect the aphids against

Ants can even pick up aphids in their mandibles ᴣm to safety, unlike humans and their cows.

Under the ants' protection, aphid thrive, sipping plant juices through their piercing-sucking mouthparts and leaving honeydew all over the leaves of the host plant, which causes sooty mold fungus to attack the plant.

Ants will even fight for possession of the aphids. When aphids took up residence on my 'Autumn Joy' sedum, two tribes of ants – one red, one black – claimed them, and went to war on the plants. Ants kept grabbing other ants and hurled them off the plant.

The best way to deal with a situation like this – well, besides sitting down and watching the show – is to get the plant away from the ants, rob the aphids of protection, and allow natural predators to help you finish off the aphids.

I poured soapy water over the sedum, rubbing the leaves and stems to get all the aphids I could. A few drops of soap per gallon works just fine, and you can rinse the plant off with clear water afterward. I also poured soapy water on the anthills that I could find. Once the aphids were gone, the ant battles ceased – on that plant, anyway, since I didn't really keep track of the ants and their wars after that.

A barrier of bone meal or charcoal will keep ants at bay – but only if the barrier stays dry. If your trees have ants running aphid farms on them, spray the tree with insecticidal soap, then put a barrier of Tanglefoot around the trunk of the tree. Tanglefoot is very sticky stuff and will stop the ants in their tracks. It will also stop any other insects, and possibly your cat, though I hope your cat will not stick to the tree like the ants will.

Once the ants are gone, you can discourage aphids. A good blast of water will knock them off the plant. You can also spray them with tobacco. You can buy it as an extract that can be diluted and sprayed, or you can soak tobacco stems in warm water for 24 hours, dilute it until it's the color of weak tea, and then spray it on the undersides of leaves. Be careful in handling the tobacco stems if you're not used to tobacco, as the nicotine can be absorbed by the skin and make you light-headed.

If you fertilize your plants regularly, cut back on the nitrogen. This element, which plants use to produce new growth, also makes the leaves soft and juicy for insect pests. Insects will jump on a succulent plant the way you'd jump on a juicy steak (or a sweet, juicy apple if you're a vegetarian).

Finally, be observant, check your plants carefully, and know what's going on in the garden. Catch aphids and other insect pests before they get out of hand, and that will give you peace of mind in the long run.

PERENNIAL RECOMMENDATIONS

Coneflowers – Great Prairie Plants for the Garden

Coneflowers, or Echinacea, are daisy-shaped, with purple petals that slope down from the center -- the flower looks like a badminton shuttlecock. And yes, this is the same Echinacea that you see in health-food stores that allegedly boost the immune system. (I just say "allegedly" because I haven't looked up the scientific studies on this yet.) The plants grow to be around 2 to 3 feet tall, and are heat- and drought-tolerant. Coneflowers are great plants for your garden, especially if you keep forgetting to go outside and water.

They, like other prairie dwellers such as liatris and black-eyed Susans, don't mind dry conditions at all -- they're used to drought. The ancestors of these plants have lived on the vast, treeless prairies of the Great Plains for generations, despite drought and thunderstorms and stampeding buffalo herds.

Coneflowers like full sun. A little light shade may help keep the colors in the petals from fading over time, but keep in mind that the plant may not bear as many flowers in shade as they would in full sun.

Coneflowers have a long blooming time -- approximately from June to September -- and the flowers have a scent of honey. Do be sure to cut off old flowers, however, which will turn black.

Coneflowers occasionally get powdery mildew or leaf spots, but generally the plants are bug- and disease-free. Their foliage, however, is not the most attractive, so you might set the plants behind a few shorter-growing plants to hide their leaves.

There are several different kinds of coneflowers to choose from at the nursery. Most commonly sold is *Echinacea purpurea* -- purpurea being the Latin word for purple. This coneflower has a prickly orange center and purple petals.

The Orange Meadowbrite coneflower stands out with its bright orange petals. Also available is 'Twilight,' 'Sunset,' and 'Sundown' – all orange – and 'Sunrise,' which is yellow. Yummy!

There are a few varieties of coneflower that might be available through seed catalogs, such as *E. pallida*, the pale purple coneflower. The flower actually leans more toward pink than purple, and its petals are not as stiffly starched as *E. purpurea*.

Coneflower is a great plant for attracting butterflies, so you might grow it in a butterfly garden with butterfly bush, sage, zinnias, and other butterfly-attracting plants. Or you might grow it in a prairie garden, mixed in with liatris and ornamental grasses such as switchgrass or maiden grass.

Plant coneflowers 1-1/2 to 2 feet apart. They will eventually grow out in clumps and fill in the area around them. Give them their space and they'll give you their blooms.

PERENNIAL GERANIUMS

May showers bring June flowers, but this is ridiculous. I am praying that this incessant rain stops for a few days. It's no fun having all of these plants all ready to go and being unable to plant them. Also, a lot of us have to worry about floods. The Noah's Ark variety, that is.

Some of the plants I'd like to get into the ground are perennial geraniums. They are in the same family as the annual geraniums, but the scientific name for the annuals is Pelargonium, while the scientific name for the perennials is Geranium. British people call the annual geraniums pelargoniums, which is an awfully good idea – though this idea has never caught on in the States.

The perennial geraniums are very good plants and worthy of their popularity. I have a 'Johnson's Blue' geranium blooming in my yard right now with its purplish flowers. The plant itself is tidy with a low, moundlike habit, growing about 12 to 18 inches tall. Once it's done blooming, you can shear off the spent blossoms before they go to seed.

Fun fact: The wild geranium is also called "wild cranesbill" because the seed pods really do look like crane bills.

'Johnson's Blue' has a long bloom-life, which I like. And if you deadhead the plant when it is done blooming, they should bloom again.

Other perennial geraniums are waiting for you to discover them. 'Ballerina,' with its pink flowers veined in red, is a dainty geranium (and tough, like the ballerinas it was named for) and *Geranium sanguineum,* with its brilliant magenta flowers. The word *sanguineum* comes from the Latin word for "blood."

Perennial geraniums even grow wild here in area forests. A common Missouri species is *Geranium maculatum,* which grows quite tall and blooms in late May. It's more scraggly than the domesticated geraniums, but is easy to grow and can spread nicely.

The Pelargoniums, the annual geraniums, are lovely, and there are many new varieties and selections hitting the market. But the perennial geraniums make a reliable, colorful splash in the garden every May and June.

MULTIFLORA BOUQUET ASTER

ASTERS: A NUISANCE OR A BEAUTY?

I used to think that asters were weedy plants, something too wild for the garden, though they looked great mixed in with a field of goldenrod.

Then one year I worked at a greenhouse potting up bare-root plants. After we potted the aster roots, I picked through the leavings and got some root bits. Much to my astonishment that fall, every microscopic bit, if it had a bud on it, came up with a vengeance, though what a pretty vengeance!

The asters I have are New England asters, a native species that is widely distributed. These have daisy-like flowers with lavender petals, and they bloom like mad through the fall, much to the delight of all the bugs that frequent the flowers for nectar.

In fall, a whole slew of fascinating bugs will drop by for liquid refreshment: butterflies, including sulfurs, skippers, and monarchs; tiny bees with saddlebags of pollen on their legs; curious little wasps; moths; and soldier beetles.

Once a blue damselfly, a dragonfly that's thin as a sewing needle, swung down over the flowers, not for nectar but to catch the nectar-drinkers: The principal food of dragonflies is bugs.

Asters will spread. One of the aster clumps has been busy growing up the little slope at the back of my garden. Some varieties of asters get a little wild – which is why they're often looked at as weeds. Asters spread through underground runners, so you don't realize they're spreading until it's too late. Also, the native species, which include the New England and New York varieties, will reseed like mad, so keep that in mind when you grow them.

The New England and New York varieties will grow true to seed if you want more plants. However, if you buy the hybrid aster varieties, such as 'Harrington's Pink,' 'Alma Potschke,' 'Marie Ballard,' or 'Crimson Brocade,' pull up the seedlings. The plants that grow from these seedlings won't look as nice as the original.

If your asters start taking over in your garden, keep them within bounds by pulling or digging out the new shoots, or divide the plants. Some divide their asters every year to keep them within bounds; some divide them every few years.

Don't divide asters in the fall when they're busy flowering and setting seed. Do this in the spring, when they're concerned with root and leaf development.

So, some call asters weeds. But even the regal calla lily is considered a weed in Africa, because the plant clogs up waterways. It just depends on how you look at it.

DOUBLE-DUTY PERENNIALS – PLANTS WITH COLORFUL LEAVES
(For some reason these are all shade plants)

An amazing number of new and intriguing perennials swamp the market every spring. It's hard to wade through all the choices and settle on only a few — after all, there's only so much space in the garden for new plants. But many perennials have been doing double duty by adding color, not only through flowers, but also through foliage, which now comes in neat colors or variegations.

Chartreuse cuties

A good spring perennial with colorful leaves is Dicentra 'Gold Heart,' which is an old-fashioned bleeding heart with screaming chartreuse foliage. Keep in mind that the whole plant will die back in early to mid-summer, so the foliage won't be permanent – but it looks good while it lasts.

A lot of chartreuse plants are hitting the market, such as coral bells (Heuchera) 'Lime Rickey,' an 8-inch-tall chartreuse plant with ruffled leaves and tiny white flowers. Veronica 'Aztec Gold' is another chartreuse cutie. It's a short plant, good as a ground cover or rock-garden plant, which has blue flower stalks in late spring. The foliage is chartreuse in part shade or gold in full sun, so you can play with it. Tradescantia, or spiderwort, 'Sweet Kate' has golden foliage and the big, three-petaled dark-blue flowers in late spring. These are related to dayflowers, which have the blue flowers and are such weeds, so you know the Tradescantia will do just FINE in the garden. Fortunately, it's less invasive.

The Tradescantia and the Dicentra have cousin species that are native to Missouri, (dayflowers for the Tradescantia and Dutchman's breeches for the Dicentra) which is very helpful. Generally, if you have a native relative to the plant in your garden, then you have a pretty good idea that these particular plants will do fine with your local climate. I don't have time for wimpy plants. If they can't take what nature throws at them, they can go away somewhere and wilt.

Variegated selections

Sedums, both the tall, fall-blooming varieties as well as the small ground covers, have an incredible number of variegated varieties, as well as selections with leaves in maroon, or silver, or gold. 'Mutrona' has a subtle hint of pink among the green. 'Frosty Morn' has a green leaf edged with white, while 'Purple Emperor' has dark burgundy foliage with dark pink flowers.

Coral Bells and their fancy-leaved brethren

Heuchera, aka Coral Bells, provide a dizzying array of foliage color. You can find brown-black foliage on 'Black

Pearl,' reddish-cinnamon on 'Cinnamon Curls,' or maroon and red on 'Fire Chief.' You can find Heuchera in almost any color of the rainbow – lime, chartereuse, burgundy, caramel, maroon edged with yellow – the list is just about endless. All of these coral bells also sports its delicate, bell-like flowers on stems that reach high above the plants. The flowers are often red, but also show up in shades of pink and white in early summer. These make good edging plants and are very tidy as well.

Not only do you have the fancy foliage of the Heuchera, but you also have a coral bells relative called x Heucherella – a hybrid which is a cross between Heuchera and Tiarella. (The x in front of Heucherella means that this plant is a hybrid of two different genera. This is very rare in the plant world.) x Heucherella, also called foam-flower or foamy bells, sports many different foliage colors, but also takes its cut-leaf shape from the Tiarella side of its family.

All three plants – Heuchera, Tiarella, and x Heucherella – prefer shade, though they'll be fine with partial or light shade. Some Heuchera do fine in full sun.

Rodgersia and Astilbes: Two great tastes that taste great together.
(Note: Please do not actually eat these plants.)
Rodgersia is a member of the Saxifrage family that likes moist conditions. Some varieties of this plant, notably 'Bronze Peacock' and 'Chocolate Wing,' have dark maroon or bronze foliage along with the green, though full sun will bring out the best leaf color. Be sure to keep the soil moist with these for best results; they'll even take boggy conditions if you have 'em. They also have large flower spikes similar to Astilbe (actually, these two plants are closely related).

Rodgeria is slow-growing but gets massive after three to five years' growth.

Astilbes are another shade plant (we are getting lots of shade plants here) that can sport colorful leaves. 'Color Flash' starts out with green leaves which morph into burgundy and purple as they mature. Its blossom spikes are white. There's also a 'Color Flash Lime' with bright lime leaves. Astilbe 'Key West' has burgundy leaves with spikes of raspberry blossoms. ('Key Largo' is another Astilbe variety, but these have the regular dark green foliage – don't get them mixed up.)

Astilbe was a favorite even back in the olden days.

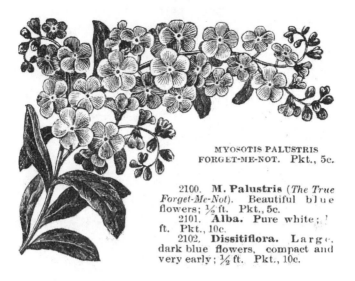

MYOSOTIS PALUSTRIS
FORGET-ME-NOT. Pkt., 5c.

2100. **M. Palustris** (*The True
Forget-Me-Not*). Beautiful blue
flowers; ½ ft. Pkt., 5c.
2101. **Alba.** Pure white;
ft. Pkt., 10c.
2102. **Dissitiflora.** Large,
dark blue flowers, compact and
very early; ½ ft. Pkt., 10c.

Several plants with sky-blue flowers

Brunnera macrophylla – also called False Forget-Me-Not, or Siberian Bugloss – is another great shade plant with variegated leaves. (It can take a little sun but the leaves might scorch a little.) You can find varieties with golden-yellow leaves, silvery leaves with green veins, all-out silver leaves, and green leaves with a wide white margin around their outer edges. Brunnera bears a cloud of baby blue flowers in mid-spring that last about a month. This plant makes a great groundcover, slowly spreading over time, with kidney-shaped leaves that are similar in shape to wild ginger, but more showy – and the flowers are much more showier than those of wild ginger, which bears little brownish blossoms underneath the leaves, almost at soil level. Anyway, I'm always a sucker for blue flowers, and Brunnera has these in spades.

Brunnera macrophylla 'Jack Frost' has silvery leaves veined with green that will light up any shady place from spring until fall. 'Silver Heart' has broad, silvery leaves, while 'Dawson's White' has a wide, white margin on the leaves.

Another shade denizen with sky blue flowers is Pulmonaria, also known as Lungwort. This little shade perennial got its odd name because the green leaves thickly spotted with white were said to resemble diseased lungs. Hey, don't look at me, I didn't come up with this stuff. But these leaves can really brighten up a shade garden. I particularly love the blooms, which are dainty bells of mingled pink and blue, or sometimes deep purple, all of which are beautiful, rich shades of colors.

Myosotis, the original forget-me-nots, does have a variegated variety, *Myosotis palustris* 'Variegata' (also named *M. scorpioides* 'Variegata'), but it seems to be available only in the U.K. and the E.U. at this time.

Ligularias

Ligularias are not a plant I've worked with much over the years, but I have heard good things about it, and its tall spikes of yellow flowers looks good in the back of the borders in mid to late summer.

There are two kinds of flowers on Ligularias – clusters of flowers that resemble black-eyed Susans (this kind grows to

be two or three feet tall), or spikes of yellow flowers, which grows five or six feet. These are shade plants in hotter areas (in the north, they'll take some sun) and prefer a moist, even boggy, soil near ponds.

'Osiris Cafe Noir' is a dwarf Ligularia ("dwarf" in this context means "it's two feet tall!") has foliage that emerges as burgundy and fades to a dark olive green. 'King Kong' Ligularias have purple-black leaves that fade to burgundy, and the leaves are 16 inches across!

Hostas

Hostas are the old guard, as far as variegated leaves go. One of my friends used to collect hosta varieties. She had these teeny little hostas that would fit into a teacup, all the way up to some hostas about as big as elephants. Small elephants, but still. Even back then, hostas had many different types of variegation in their leaves, most of which in variations of yellow or white and green. Some hostas have yellow-gold or chartreuse leaves; some have bluish-silver leaves; some are nearly all white or yellow with a touch of green outlining the leaves. Hostas thrive in shade and have white or purple blossoms in late summer.

You can also underplant bulbs under hostas. The tulips come up first for a bright show of color, and then when the display is over, the hosta leaves come up and help to hide the spent foliage.

Hostas have of course been popular in shade gardens with their variegated colors. "Jane" is a real knockout with butter-yellow leaves edged with green. "Earth Angel" is subtler, a big, green-leafed plant edged with yellow. It gets 30 inches tall and 2 feet wide, so give it room. "Cheatin Heart" is a little gold-leafed hosta that's 8 inches tall, while

"Blue Cadet" has tidy blue leaves and is as tough as nails. "Zippity Do Dah" has tidy, slightly wavy leaves with a nice white edge.

"Revolution" is a neat hosta: it was developed from "Patriot" and "Loyalist," so it has a margin of green that looks like it has been painted on a yellow leaf with bold strokes. Inside the yellow are speckles of green. It's a standout.

Ajuga

Ajuga is a vigorous groundcover will bear purple, pink, or white blossoms on short flower spikes in spring. But the rest of the year, and even into winter, their variegated leaves put on a good show of color of purple, green, and white, which darkens and becomes more vibrant as the temperatures drop. In mild climates, Ajuga is an evergreen perennial, which means that it doesn't die back to the ground and even keeps its colorful foliage for most of the winter. (Protip: Plant tulip or narcissus bulbs under the Ajuga, and they'll add to the color display in early spring. Then when the foliage dies back, the ajuga should be able to hide the dying foliage somewhat while still putting on a nice color show.)

Man, I haven't even scratched the surface on these shade plant sweethearts. How about Lamium, a little groundcover that's a member of the mint family, with its silver-edged leaves? Or Periwinkle! Bergenia! Cimicifuga, which has dark burgundy leaves and gets nice and tall in your shade garden! Autumn ferns and painted ferns! The list goes on and on.

MONTH-BY-MONTH CHECKLIST

January

Add more mulch to your plants if necessary. Do you have leaf piles from last fall that are still out of control? Run the lawn mower over the leaves to chop them and use them as mulch. I got ten big bags of leaves from my grandma, and about seven bags from my neighbors, spread them all over the garden, then mowed and mowed. It took about an hour, but the big heaps of leaves became a good layer of mulch.

Now I wish I had more leaves. The ground under the leaf mulch doesn't freeze as brick-solid as unmulched ground, and you can see that the earthworms have been busy under the leaves – and the more earthworms you have, the healthier your soil is.

Water your outside plants, which lose moisture through their stems and their buds. Of course, do this when the temps are above 32 degrees!

Wash your pots and trays to get ready for seeding plants next month. Use hot, soapy water, then rinse with a mild bleach solution and let them dry.

You can still plant spring-flowering bulbs any time when the ground is not frozen. They might not bloom this year, but they'll have forgiven you by next year (if the voles haven't eaten them by then).

February

My yard is lousy. When I take care of the city's gardens all day, the last thing I want to do when I get home is clean up my yard, so I go inside to write novels instead. The yard has no grass, because Marcus, my awesome little bulldog, likes to show off his masculinity by kicking turf in all directions.

This is a good time to rake leaves, trim the yews, and clear away dead perennials and iris stems. A lot of winter weeds can be pulled now -- some of the low-growing weeds already have little blue flowers. Try to keep up with these weeds in the perennial garden, and throw down mulch where your garden needs it.

This is a good time to prune trees (it's never a good time to top trees) and clean up for the upcoming season. Spring's coming up fast!

Clean and sharpen your gardening tools. Sand off any rough spots or splinters on wooden handles and apply a coat of linseed oil. Buy new gardening gloves if you've worn holes in the fingers again.

March

Well, December was slow, January was pretty much dead, and there was a little action in February – but now it's March, and my gardener's blood is pumping again. The rest of you might feel it, too. At last, we can start seeds and till our gardens, not just kick miserably at the frozen ground.

March means that area greenhouses have been jumping into action. Growers have started their seed flats and should be receiving shipments of zonal geranium cuttings. (Digression: Since zonal and ivy geranium varieties are patented, growers aren't allowed to take cuttings for profit the way they can with seed geraniums. So, growers have to buy these geraniums as slips, which are basically rooted cuttings, and then pot them up. That's why zonal geraniums are more expensive than seed geraniums.)

Toward the end of March, you can look forward to seeing garden centers filled with plants: lavender and delphiniums and butterfly bush and 18 different kinds of sage and coneflowers and artemesia. Ain't it great? I am looking forward to cruising around the nurseries, even though I don't dare plant anything until mid to late April.

I have been happily surrounded by plants in the greenhouse, however. One of the good things about being city horticulturist is having a greenhouse to play with. In January I took a bunch of geranium cuttings. A good man, just before the first October frost, gave the city 40 geraniums, since he had no place to keep them through the winter. Nearly all of them survived. One or two died of frost damage, but the rest are blooming their heads off, and the cuttings I took in January are getting pretty big.

Recently, though, I've been busy with all the new stuff – potting up the bare-root perennials.

Bare-root perennials!

We got a pile of bare-root perennials in, so I've been mixing soil and potting those up. Bare-root perennials are just roots with a crown with a little green on top. (The crown of a plant is where the roots meet the stem – the place from which all the green parts grows up and all the brown parts grow down, mostly.)

I look over each mass of roots, trim the roots slightly to encourage them to branch out, and snip off dead bits, if any. Once these are all trimmed and ready to go, you get a stack of pots and set them off to the side. Grab a pot, scoop a little soil in it, put the perennial in the pot and hold it where you want it to go (that is, in the middle of the pot with the crown just above where the top of the soil will be), then scoop soil in around it until the crown sits just above soil level. Gently firm in the soil, add extra soil if necessary, then set the finished pot aside and move on to the next pot. When you're done potting up the bare-root perennials, set them on the greenhouse floor (or table, depending on your setup) and water in the little plants. And there you have it.

So the potted bare-root perennials take up one part of the greenhouse, and the potted geraniums another part. Then the seed flats, about 36 of them, take up a good chunk of the greenhouse tables. I seeded the cosmos on Friday, and by Monday they had already germinated. I can't wait until they get big enough to transplant.

I'm trying to stay as far ahead of schedule as I can, lest the weeds overwhelm the city garden beds. (This time, however, I've been throwing down pre-emergents to keep the weed seeds from even sprouting.) If I can keep the weeds down before I plant, then mulch the new plants in well, the gardens in the park should look very good once the plants start growing.

April

This is a good time to start watering perennials, since the winter's been so dry. A good watering will help them gear up for spring.

If you're really itching to do some garden work, divide and move some perennials (at least, those that need it). If the ground is not frozen, perennials should have no problem with their relocation. Give them plenty of space to grow and flourish, water them well, and give them some mulch to protect them from any freezes we might have. Because you know that the freezes will hit between now and May (usually after you plant a bunch of tender stuff).

It's an especially good time for spring clean-up. Rake the leaves, trim the yews, and clear away dead perennials and iris stems. A lot of winter weeds can be pulled now -- some of the low-growing weeds already have little blue flowers. You can also use vinegar to kill off some of the annual weeds such as henbit (the purple flowering one) and chickweed (the one you can eat). Plain white vinegar, right out of the kitchen, will burn down annual and perennial weeds. The perennial weeds will grow back, so keep hitting them until they die from exhaustion.

You can also buy herbicidal vinegar in some garden or retail stores. Keep in mind, however, that the herbicidal vinegar contains 10 to 20 percent acid – it can burn your eyes and skin. Always wear eye and skin protection when using this vinegar. It's definitely not the same stuff you'd put on your salad.

Put supports next to your top-heavy peonies and dahlias.

Cut back butterfly bushes (Buddleia) to six inches above the soil line.

Give your compost pile a good mixing to wake it up. A mini-tiller works great for this.

May

I want to buy about a half-million perennials, but unfortunately that would result in my family being forced to live on cat food for the rest of our days. Well, you can't have everything.

For shady locations, I want to get my hands on 'Pine Knot' Helleborus, or Lenten Rose. It blooms in winter for months, and the flowers come in many millions of marvelous shades.

I've been grabbing up Filipendula, or Queen of the Prairie, Gaillardias, Hostas, Russian Sage "Little Spire," Coral

Bells, and Yarrow "Coronation Gold." I like Gaillardias. When you drive through eastern Oklahoma in summer, they're blooming all red and yellow among the Texas bluebonnets at the side of the road. They will bloom for months.

In the perennial garden, your late-growing plants should be finally putting in their appearance – hibiscus is one of the slowpokes. So is lavender. Finish cleaning out the leaves and the old sticks, and make a list of what needs to be replaced or divided. Weeds will be a nuisance. Get rid of them fast before they become downright noxious. Dandelions should be dug out, root and all, or they will keep returning. Put a little flag or a small label in the place where your bleeding heart plant is growing, because it will vanish soon (as it does every year) when it dies back to the ground. Then mulch, mulch, mulch. Of course!

Annuals can go into the ground, too, if you haven't already put them out.

Don't cut back the foliage for tulips, daffodils, or other spring-flowering bulbs until they die. Grandma always braided the daffodil foliage together, and that seemed to get it out of the way. Better yet, plant hostas among them if the bulbs are in a shade/part shade location. The broad leaves of the hostas will hide the spent growth.

Slugs in the hostas again? Sprinkle diatomaceous earth around plants. The diatomaceous earth (which looks like pulverized chalk) should be replaced after every rain. Also, I've discovered that chalk drawings on the sidewalk can also kill slugs. (It's not pretty.) You can also set out saucers of beer, and the slugs will crawl into them and drown. Unfortunately, raccoons like this too, and it is a bad thing to have drunken raccoons staggering and yowling outside your house at 3 a.m. (Note: this has never happened to me.)

June

Pinch back your mums after they have their first small blooms are finished. This will get you big, bushy plants, and give you more blooms in the fall.

Plant your cannas, calla lilies, and glads among your perennials now.

Thin your phlox, cutting down all but the five strongest stems on each plant. This will encourage air circulation to keep powdery mildew down.

Mix a batch of compost tea for your plants. Put several shovelfuls of compost in a burlap bag, tie the bag, and put it in a rain barrel full of water. Cover it and let it steep for a couple of weeks before using it on the plants.

Deadhead any perennials that have finished blooming. Do the same for annuals in your flowerbeds.

Rig up some kind of system to capture Japanese beetles to feed to your hens. If you don't have hens, find a place to set up a pheromone trap far from your yard to lure them out. I have seriously thought about taking a hand-held vacuum, or even a Shop-Vac, into the garden and sucking them up, because seriously, holy cow, those things are thick.

Weed! Weed!! Weed!!!

Put down a thick layer of mulch (lawn mower clippings, for instance) to keep plant roots cool, keep the weeds down, and keep the soil moist and the worms busy.

July

Keep deadheading flowers. Petunias should be pinched back before they start getting too leggy. Cut mums back one more time so they'll be ready to bloom this fall. Any spent flowers should be cut off, unless you're trying to save some seeds for next year.

Divide your irises. Throw out any soft rhizomes, or anything infested with insects. Don't cut back the leaves, though – the plant needs to keep photosynthesizing.

Pass through your gardens every week and keep up on the weeds. Throw more mulch in spots that need it.

You can dig and divide daylilies any time from now until fall.

Water! Water!! Water!!! Let the water hose soak water into the soil. Don't spritz the plants with a little mist, as that does absolutely no good. A nice, deep watering is the way to go.

Watch for pests on your plants. Often you can knock a lot of them off with a powerful spray of water from the hose. Also, spray with insecticidal soap or neem oil. Also, squish them with your fingers. Fight the war on several fronts, but in a way that doesn't harm the predatory insects that will help you stop the problem in your tracks.

Stake tall plants like delphiniums.

August

Please be careful on the hot days. If you start feeling nauseated, dizzy, or disoriented, get out of the sun immediately, drink cold water, even get into the bathtub and cool off. Heatstroke is a very real danger this time of year –

so please be safe. People have died of this. Be sure to have water out in the field with you, or, better yet, a sports drink with electrolytes, so you can stay hydrated.

Water! Water!! Water!!! Water!!!!

If this month actually cools off, this is a good time to divide your perennials. Peonies are best divided or transplanted from now until September, if they need it.

Start new perennials from seeds in your garden – you still have time for these guys to get established before frost comes.

Prepare new beds for planting by laying thick layers of cardboard right over the weeds and grass. You can do the same with a thick layer of newspapers (at least ten sheets thick). Throw mulch on top and let them sit for a month at least before planting in.

Edge the garden beds if it's not too dry.

Don't let your compost pile dry out!

PETUNIA   CYPRESS VINE   ESCHSCHOLTZIA   BALSAM   PHLOX   ASTER

September

There have been a few days that have been so downright cool that I think that it's already autumn. Maybe there's hope for us yet.

Here are a few tasks to take care of now that the weather's finally cooling down, to prepare the garden for the fall months and their last gasp before winter comes in. (Feels strange to think about winter right now, though.)

Replenish your perennial garden by getting new plants. Stop by your local nursery and buy plants in the fall – in September and especially October, as they will sell plants for cheap. Generally any perennials left at this time of year are either thrown out or put into storage for the winter – and any plants they sell won't be taking up space in the holding shed.

These fall plants won't be as pretty as those you will see in the spring – but you can get a lot more of them. What's more, you'll have them in the ground, already growing, next spring. Then you can really start to fill in the gaps.

'Tis the season to plant bulbs. If you have moles, you'll have to purchase lots of grit to put into the ground with the bulbs to keep rodents at bay. (The moles won't eat tulips, but the voles and mice that use the mole tunnels will.) When you dig each tulip hole, drop in a little grit, set the bulb on top, then cover the rest of the tulip with grit before burying.

This is a good time to replace plants in the perennial border. Plants are cheap this time of year. Also, planting now allows plants to get established for two growing seasons before summer hits and dries them out. Just be sure to give them a decent mulch this fall so they get through winter all right.

This is also a good time to clean up all those weeds you couldn't get to this summer. Bring along a pair of pruners for the small trees that have gotten a roothold in your gardens. Sometimes, if the ground's really wet after a good rain, and if you're really tough, you can actually pull the trees out, root and all. More often, though, you'll have to clip it at ground level. Or dig it out with a shovel so you don't have to keep cutting it year after year. Most weeds, though, shouldn't require as much horsepower to pull. There's always so many of them, that they wear you out anyway. And who likes to pull weeds?

Not me!

That's why I'm a big fan of mulch. Once you get the weeds pulled, lay down ten layers of newspapers, then cover them with a layer of straw, wood chips, etc. The areas I mulched in my garden several months ago still looks nice. The stuff I didn't mulch – well, that is going to be set on fire.

Okay, maybe not. Don't think I'm not tempted.

This is a good time of year to mulch, anyway. Soon, thanks to your deciduous trees, you'll have more mulch than you know what to do with. Start piling dead leaves over your vegetable garden for the day you can turn your lawnmower loose on them and turn them into a fine mulch. That'll be good stuff to till under when the day comes.

You can still plant perennials and trees and shrubs until the ground freezes. Just mulch them in well, of course, and keep them watered.

Take cuttings of your perennials before frost strikes them down. Find a stem that's at least 6 inches long with several healthy leaves on it. Using sharp shears, cut the stem at an angle about 1/4 inch below a node or joint.

Let the cutting dry an hour or so, then put it into the water. Don't let any leaves slip under the water's surface, for they will rot. Then, transfer the cutting into the soil when roots are 1/2 inch long.

October

I'm still waiting for the big October freeze to hit – the one that turns the marigolds black and turns the impatiens into slime. When it comes, it's time to heave a big sigh and start winter preparations.

Annuals will have to come out of the ground by the fistful. Some will survive the frosts, however – I've seen alyssum blooming through Halloween, and snapdragons blooming in November, and still green in December.

You can still plant in your garden. Put in mums, pansies, and flowering kale for a little late-season color. Some of the cold-season plants can stay in the ground, too. In the vegetable garden, you'll still have parsley, spinach, lettuce, and root vegetables, so don't pull everything up!

And of course there's still plenty of time to plant perennials, shrubs, and trees. Their roots will be in the ground, safe from winter's cold, and the roots will grow over the winter. When spring hits, these plants will pick right up and start growing, and you won't have to bother with all that spring mud and slush.

Tender bulbs.

Dig up tender bulbs like calla lilies, cannas, elephant ears, dahlias, gladiolus, etc. Separate the bulbs from the plants, let the bulbs dry out for a few days, then store them in dry peat moss in a dry, cool place, or keep them in paper bags. Be sure to label them so they don't get all mixed up next year.

November

Ooh, here comes winter. Here come the leafless trees, the sullen skies, the cold rains, and there goes the heating bill.

And thousands of people who work in nurseries or greenhouses are now out of a job.

I love winter! No, I don't.

Still, you've got to admit that if we didn't have winter, we wouldn't get the spectacular blaze of autumn leaves, or the shy new green and the smell of lilacs. You can't grow peonies in Houston (much to the dismay of my aunt, who lives there) because the southern climate doesn't give these plants the dormant period that they need to bear their lovely blooms. So maybe we should consider ourselves lucky. Maybe.

Now that your perennials have turned brown, cut them back to an inch above the soil line. Don't cut them back while they're still green, because they're trying to manufacture and store the starches they need to survive the winter.

But wait until next spring (specifically, next May) to cut back sage, lavender, or southernwood.

Mulch the garden. Then, once the ground has frozen solid, add two inches more mulch to avoid the freeze/thaw cycles that can heave plants out of the soil.

You can keep gathering mulches right now – autumn leaves, old straw bales. If you spread it out and run a mulching mower over them, you'll get a good mulch that will be a good cover for your perennials through the winter. Better yet, the earthworms will be working on these leaves through the winter.

One winter I mulched a layer of chopped leaves several inches thick over my garden. When I peeked under the leaves in February, I found that the worms had been busy, and the ground was covered with worm castings – black gold to plants. Worm castings – i.e. worm poop – is full of minerals and elements that are in a form that's very easy for roots to absorb. Organic mulches like leaves are heaven for worms – and super good for your plants.

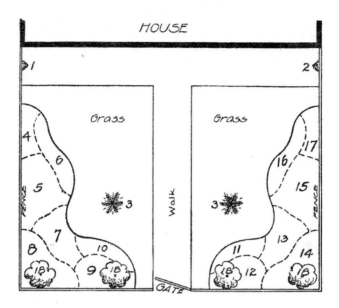

December
Plan Next Year's Garden for Best Results

So you're out in the garden, and some of the perennials look crowded, and some of the flower colors don't really match, and the astilbes are getting too much sun because their leaves are looking burned.

Bad garden day? Bad garden *year*?

Winter is a good time to remedy that. If you make a plan for next year's garden right now, you'll be ready for next year's new arrivals today.

First, look at what your garden has right now, and (this is important) make notes. Do the daylilies need dividing? Has the creeping Charlie crept all over the garden? Make a list of anything that requires decisive gardening action.

Then think about what you want from your garden. Is this a place where you like to putter around and try new plant varieties? Are you trying to impress the neighbors? Experiment with color? And what things would you like to do in your garden? Perhaps you'd like to have a cutting garden, or start attracting hummingbirds. Write all these ideas down, too.

Next, figure out what plants you need to grow so you can have the garden you want. If you want a hummingbird garden, look through catalogs or the local nursery and see what kind of red-flowered plants you like. Also, if you come across plants you especially like, write those down, too. Clip plant pictures from catalogs and tape them into a notebook, or keep a file on your computer with plant pictures in them. These pictures are especially useful: when it comes time to make your design, you can use these pictures to match colors to get the effect you want.

Once the plant list is done, think about how well these plants would fit in with the plants you already have. If your garden is filled with Monet pastels, then adding fire-engine red plants probably would be problematic.

Then it's time for the big step: drawing a plan. Measure your garden. To keep your plan simple, let one-half inch equal one foot. Draw the outline of the garden on your paper. Protip: Once you have this step finished to your satisfaction, take this paper to the copier and make several copies, and use these as the rough drafts of your garden design.

IRIS AND HELIOTROPES.

Now play with that outline. Consider the height and width of these plants. Keep short plants in front and tall plants in back, and use those pictures you've clipped (whether out of a magazine or found on the internet) to make sure the colors match. Do you want soft colors, such as purple catmint, pink petunias, and silver Artemisia? Or do you want a fiesta of red salvia and "Yellow Boy" marigolds?

Also, consider when your perennials bloom. You may love purple asters and pink sea thrift, but that color pairing won't be happening, because the asters bloom in fall and the sea thrift blooms in spring.

Now that you know what you want from your garden, start playing around with what you already have out there. Thanks to your lists, you know what plants you want to keep and what plants you need to give away. Do your dividing and moving work now, while you can see the results. That will give you more time in spring for planting the new flowers – and for enjoying the results.

THE END

FREE PREVIEWS OF MY OTHER GARDENING BOOKS

Here's a preview of *Don't Throw in the Trowel: Vegetable Gardening Month by Month.*

Two things:

First: You know more about gardening than you think.

Second: A garden – the soil – plants – all of these are very forgiving. When it comes down to it, you can make a lot of mistakes and still come out with good results.

Don't Throw in the Trowel! Vegetable Gardening Month by Month *includes info on seeds, transplanting, growing, and harvesting, as well as diseases, garden pests, and organic gardening. I also talk about garden prep, because a good plan, a garden notebook, and a little off-season work will save you a lot of trouble down the road.*

I've worked in horticulture for 20 years: in landscape design and installation, as a greenhouse tech, perennial manager, and city horticulturist & rosarian. This book shares what I've learned so far.

Preview from Don't Throw in the Trowel

Save Time and Trouble With Garden Journals

When I worked as a municipal horticulturist, I took care of twelve high-maintenance gardens, and a number of smaller ones, over I-don't-know-how-many square miles of city, plus several hundred small trees, an insane number of shrubs, a greenhouse, and whatever else the bosses threw at me. I had to find a way to stay organized besides waking up at 3 a.m. to make extensive lists. My solution: keep a garden journal.

Vegetable gardeners with an organized journal can take control of production and yields. Whether you have a large garden or a small organic farm, it certainly helps to keep track of everything in order to beat the pests, make the most of your harvest, and keep up with spraying and fertilizing.

Keeping a garden journal reduces stress because your overtaxed brain won't have to carry around all those lists. It saves time by keeping you focused. Writing sharpens the mind, helps it to retain more information, and opens your eyes to the world around you.

My journal is a small five-section notebook, college ruled, and I leave it open to the page I'm working on at the time. The only drawback with a spiral notebook is that after a season or two I have to thumb through a lot of pages to find an earlier comment. A small three-ring binder with five separators would do the trick, too. If you wish, you can take out pages at the end of each season and file them in a master notebook.

I keep two notebooks – one for ornamentals and one for vegetables. However, you might prefer to pile everything into one notebook. Do what feels comfortable to you.

These are the five sections I divide my notebooks into – though you might use different classifications, or put them in different orders. Don't sweat it; this ain't brain surgery. Feel free to experiment. You'll eventually settle into the form that suits you best.

First section: To-do lists.

This is pretty self-explanatory: you write a list, you cross off almost everything on it, you make a new list.

When I worked as horticulturist, I did these lists monthly. I'd visit all the gardens I took care of. After looking at anything left unfinished on the previous month's list, and looking at the garden to see what else needed to be done, I made a new, comprehensive list.

Use one page of the to-do section for reminders of things you need to do next season. If it's summer, and you think of some chores you'll need to do this fall, make a FALL page and write them down. Doing this has saved me lots of headaches.

Second section: Reference lists.

These are lists that you'll refer back to on occasion.

For example, I'd keep a list of all the yews in the parks system that needed trimmed, a list of all gardens that needed weekly waterings, a list of all places that needed sprayed for bagworms, a list of all the roses that needed to be babied, etc.

I would also keep my running lists in this section, too – lists I keep adding to.

For instance, I kept a list of when different vegetables were ready for harvest – even vegetables I didn't grow, as my friends and relatives reported to me. Then when I made a plan for my veggie garden, I would look at the list to get an idea of when these plants finished up, and then I could figure out when I could take them out and put in a new crop. I also had a list of "seed-to-harvest" times, so I could give each crop enough time to make the harvest date before frost.

You can also keep a wish list – plants and vegetables you'd like to have in your garden.

Third section: Tracking progress.

This is a weekly (or, "whenever it occurs to me to write about it") section as well.

If you plant seeds in a greenhouse, keep track of what seeds you order, when you plant them, when they germinate, how many plants you transplant (and how many survive to maturity), and so forth.

When you finish up in the greenhouse, use these pages to look back and record your thoughts – "I will never again try to start vinca from seeds! Never!! Never!!!" Then you don't annoy yourself by forgetting and buying vinca seeds next year.

You can do the same thing when you move on to the vegetable garden – what dates you tilled the ground, planted the seeds, when they germinated, and so forth. Make notes on yields and how everything tasted. "The yellow crooknecks were definitely not what I'd hoped for. Try yellow zucchini next year."

Be sure to write a vegetable garden overview at season's end, too. "Next year, for goodness' sake, get some 8-foot poles for the beans! Also, drive the poles deeper into the ground so they don't fall over during thunderstorms."

During the winter, you can look back on this section and see ways you can improve your yields and harvest ("The dehydrator worked great on the apples!"), and you can see which of your experiments worked.

Fourth section: Details of the natural world.

When keeping a journal, don't limit yourself to what's going on in your garden. Track events in the natural world, too. Write down when the poplars start shedding cotton or when the Queen's Anne Lace blooms.

You've heard old gardening maxims such as "plant corn when oak leaves are the size of a squirrel's ear," or "prune roses when the forsythia blooms." If the spring has been especially cold and everything's behind, you can rely on nature's cues instead of a calendar when planting or preventing disease outbreaks.

Also, by setting down specific events, you can look at the journal later and say, "Oh, I can expect little caterpillars to attack the indigo plant when the Johnson's Blue geranium is blooming." Then next year, when you notice the buds on your geraniums, you can seek out the caterpillar eggs and squish them before they hatch. An ounce of prevention, see?

When I read back over this section of the journal, patterns start to emerge. I noticed that Stargazer lilies bloom just as the major heat begins. This is no mere coincidence: It's happened for the last three years! So now when I see the large buds, I give the air conditioner a quick checkup.

Fifth section: Notes and comments.

This is more like the journal that most people think of as being a journal – here, you just talk about the garden, mull over how things are looking, or grouse about those supposedly blight-resistant tomatoes that decided to be contrary and keel over from blight.

I generally put a date on each entry, then ramble on about any old thing. You can write a description of the garden at sunset, sketch your peppers, or keep track of the habits of bugs you see crawling around in the plants. This ain't art, this is just fun stuff (which, in the end, yields great dividends).

Maybe you've been to a garden talk on the habits of Asian melons and you need a place to put your notes. Put them here!

This is a good place to put garden plans, too. Years later I run into them again, see old mistakes I've made, and remember neat ideas I haven't tried yet.

Get a calendar.

Then, when December comes, get next year's calendar and the gardening journal and sit down at the kitchen table. Using last year's notes, mark on the calendar events to watch out for -- when the tomatoes first ripen, when the summer heat starts to break, and when you expect certain insects to attack. In the upcoming year, you just look at the calendar and say, "Well, the squash bugs will be hatching soon," so you put on your garden gloves and start smashing the little rafts of red eggs on the plants.

A garden journal can be a fount of information, a source of memories, and most of all, a way to keep organized. Who thought a little spiral notebook could do so much?

PREVIEW OF
ROSE TO THE OCCASION: AN EASY-GROWING GUIDE TO ROSE GARDENING

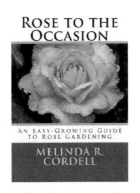

Roses are the Queen of Flowers. They're beautiful, fragrant, and elegant - and roses require all the pampering of a real Queen, don't they?

Actually, they don't!

Rose gardening can be easy and pleasant. I've worked 25 years in horticulture and cared for over 300 roses in a public rose garden when I was municipal horticulturist. I found ways to keep rose gardening fussbudgetry to a minimum while growing vigorous roses that bloomed their heads off. Rose to the Occasion: An Easy-Growing Guide to Rose Gardening shares tricks and shortcuts that rosarians use, plus simple ways you can keep up with your to-do list in the rose garden.

Gardeners of all skill levels will find this book helpful, whether they be beginning gardeners or old rosarians, whether they have a green thumb or a brown thumb.

Rose to the Occasion *is the ultimate resource for any rose gardener, or anybody in need of good gardening advice. Roses are filled with romance, history, color, and fragrance. Grow some. They are worth it.*

INTRODUCTION TO
ROSE TO THE OCCASION

When I started working as city horticulturist, I took care of a bunch of gardens around the city, including the big Krug Park rose garden. It included a bunch of the usual scrawny tea roses, some shrub roses, and a bunch of bare ground.

I was more of a perennials gal, but when I looked at the roses, some of them were really nice. The 'Carefree Delight' roses were covered with rumpled pink blossoms. There was a tall 'Mr. Lincoln' rose and some 'Double Delights' that smelled amazing. A bunch of 'Scarlet Meidilands' were really putting on a blooming show, with tiny scarlet flowers cascading all over them. Not shabby at all.

I started taking care of the roses, but I noticed that a lot of the 'Scarlet Meidilands' were sprouting odd growths. Most of the new growth looked fine, with bronzed, flat leaves that looked attractive. But some of the new growth was markedly different – skinny, stunted leaves with pebbled surfaces, and hyperthorny canes that were downright rubbery. The blossoms on these shoots were crinkled and didn't open worth a darn.

I hollered at Charles Anctil, a Master Rosarian with the American Rose Society. We'd known each other since 1992 when we both worked at the Old Mill Nursery. He'd been working with roses for a good 50 years, and he knows his stuff. At any rate, Charles looked over the roses and told me that those roses, and others, had rose rosette virus, a highly contagious disease, and a death sentence for a rose. Every one of those roses had to come out. He couldn't believe the extent of the damage. He said that he had never seen so many roses infected by rose rosette in one place.

Oh great! Why do I get to be the lucky one?

I dug up many roses that spring. That winter, I got a work crew and dug up 50 more. I had to replace all those roses, so I started researching new varieties.

As city horticulturist with no staff, I was already running like hell everywhere I went, so I wanted roses that wouldn't wilt or croak or wrap themselves in blackspot every time I looked at them cross-eyed. I wanted tough roses, roses that took heat and drought and bug attacks and zombie apocalypses with aplomb and would still come out looking great and covered with scented blossoms. (And the blossoms HAD to be scented – there was no two ways about that.)

I started reading rose catalogs. I talked to Charles some more, which is always fun. Somewhere along the way, I got obsessed. I immersed myself in roses. That's how I learn – I get excited about a subject and start reading everything in sight about it, as if it's a mini-course in school. I read about antique roses, which were making a comeback. Different rose breeders, most notably David Austin, were crossing modern varieties with old varieties and to get roses that combined the best of the new and the old. Other breeders were creating roses that were tough and disease-resistant, such as the 'Knock-Out' landscape rose, which now you see everywhere.

I planted some antique roses, and they looked great. I planted more. The rose garden was starting to look spiffy, even though I still had to take roses out every year due to the rose rosette virus. I even tucked in some annuals and perennials around the garden to doll up the place when the roses conked out in July and August.

Roses are amazing plants. Many old roses have a long and storied history. Some species that were growing during the time of the Pyramids are still blooming today. And these roses are attractive and fragrant. What could be better?

Some people say that you can't grow roses organically. I say you can. I did use a few chemicals when I was a horticulturist, but that was because I had a huge list of things to do in a limited amount of time. I used Round Up for spot-weeding (a tiny squirt for each weed, just enough to wet the leaves), a systemic granular fungicide to keep up with blackspot, and Miracle-Gro as part of the fertilizing regimen for convenience.

If you choose to use chemicals, use them responsibly. Don't spray them and expect the problem to be fixed. They work best when you combine them with other control methods. I'll give you an example that's not rose-related. I had a mandevilla plant in the greenhouse that had a huge mealybug problem. (Mealybugs are a small, white insect that sucks out plant juices. The young bugs look like bits of cotton. Picture to the right.) I sprayed the plant with insecticide until the leaves were dripping. The mealybugs were still there. I put a systemic insecticide around the roots of the plant and watered it in. The mealybugs didn't care.

So I just started squishing the mealybugs with my fingers, a gross job because they squirt orange goo. At that point, I didn't care. I searched them out and squashed them where they were cuddled up around buds, in the cracks of the plant, and under the leaves. I even found some on the roots just under the soil. I squished those and added a little extra potting soil. I checked the plant every other day and squished every mealybug I could find. After a while, I stopped finding them altogether. Then I fertilized the plant, and the mandevilla put out leaves like crazy and started blooming. Success!

Chemicals aren't a cure-all by any means. They're convenient, but sometimes you just have to get in and do a little hands-on work with the plant to help it along. It's a good feeling when a plant you've been working with rights itself and perks up again.

Though I'm no longer a horticulturist, I wrote this book because I have worked in horticulture for about half my life, and have a decent understanding about how the natural world works. I might possibly be just a little crazy about roses. I hope my experiences are helpful and that you're able to benefit from them – and that your roses benefit as well.

If You're a Tomato, I'll Ketchup With You: Tomato Gardening Tips and Tricks.

The National Gardening Association has found that, among vegetable gardeners, tomatoes are their favorite plant to grow. One in three Americans have a vegetable garden, and 9 out of 10 of those gardens have tomatoes in them.

Welcome to the world of tomato gardening.

There's nothing as sweet and good as a sun-warmed tomato fresh from the garden on a hot summer afternoon. It's no wonder that tomatoes are the most popular vegetable in America (though botanically, tomatoes are a fruit).

This book walks you through the steps in raising tomatoes – through starting tomato seeds, planting (and tricks for planting tomatoes early), and staking and caging tomatoes. Readers learn how to fight off diseases and insect pests, decipher the mysterious letters on a tomato tag, how to harvest tomatoes, and how to dry, can, or freeze tomatoes for next year.

With plenty of information for advanced gardeners, ready help for beginning gardeners, lots of expert knowledge, and a smidgeon of wit, If You're a Tomato will guide you in the ways of the vegetable garden with a minimum of fuss and feathers. Also with a minimum of weeding. Nobody likes weeding.

Tomato Varieties

In January and February, when spring fever is really hitting hard, those heirloom seed catalogs inspire dreams of the perfect vegetable garden and the veritable cornucopia of delicious vegetables that it will pour upon our collective tables. Not literally of course, as that would be a mess. But man, those seed catalog tomatoes. It wouldn't be so bad if the seed catalogs could offer taste samples of everything.

When I flip through the Baker Creek seed catalog, which is far and away my favorite, they offer 13 pages of tomatoes (and one page of tomatillos). And so many heirloom varieties. Who knew there was such a variety of tomatoes? Green tomatoes, orange tomatoes, pink tomatoes. Here are the purple, black, and brown tomatoes, which include Black Krim, Cherokee Purple, Paul Robeson, and True Black Brandywine. They have red tomatoes, naturally, two pages of striped tomatoes, two pages of Brad Gate's multicolored tomatoes, some of which are downright psychedelic in purples, yellows, reds, and browns. Then we have blue tomatoes (actually rich purples) and white tomatoes (a very pale yellow, like Bunnicula had been at work on them), and of course yellow tomatoes. I had a Yellow Pear tomato plant that took over half my garden. I can appreciate that kind of vigor in my plants. You can also get peach tomatoes, which have a light layer of fuzz.

Tomatoes also range in size from gigantic beefsteak tomatoes that can weigh up to a half-pound, to the smallest cherry tomato about the size of a marble. You can grow heavy-yielding hybrids or open-pollinated heirloom varieties in different colors, shades, and sizes. You can choose early varieties that set fruit when it's cool outside, mid-season varieties, and late-maturing varieties that will give you the biggest fruits but take 80 to 90 days to do it. Sometimes you'll need about 120 days to get a decent harvest, but hey, at least you get tomatoes!

Tomatoes are so versatile and so good. You can cook them a million different ways or you can eat them, sun-warmed and delicious, straight off the vine. Some people grab a cherry tomato, a leaf of basil, and a slice of mozzarella cheese, and eat them like that.

Determinate vs. indeterminate

I've known about these two different kinds of tomatoes for decades and yet I still can't keep them straight in my head. It's like the difference between flammable and inflammable, kind of.

Determinate tomatoes produce fruit at the ends of their branches. These will stop growing when they are still pretty short.

Indeterminate tomatoes bear fruit along their stems, which keep growing and growing and growing.

If you want a little short tomato to grow in a pot on your patio, get a determinate one.

If you want a Godzilla tomato to take over the world, get an indeterminate one.

Starting Tomatoes from Seed

If you start tomatoes from seed, it's best to start them inside, whether on a window sill or in a cold frame. At any rate, tomatoes need a soil temperature of at least 60 degrees to germinate, though they prefer warmer temperatures, up to 80 degrees. It's a sure bet that your outdoor soil temperature aren't going to get that high any time soon!

Tomato seeds need to be started six to eight weeks before the last frost date.

You can start Early Girl tomatoes (or any early tomato variety) under lights as early as February, then, when the weather is mild enough, transplant to the garden with a Wall o' Waters to help protect the plants against all the frosts.

Traditionally, in Missouri, zone 5, this date has been May 15. With global warming as it is, that date can be moved back to May 1, and even earlier. (Old gardening wisdom is always helpful, but still needs to be updated from time to time.)

So get out your calendar and count back six or eight weeks from your frost date, and that's your sowing date. (Protip: Keep a gardening calendar and notebook where you write down things like sowing dates, the dates you see frost, etc., and use them next winter when you're planning for the next planting year.)

Next, line up your planting containers. Whether you use old egg cartons, Solo cups, flower pots, have them scrubbed (well, don't scrub the egg cartons) if you're reusing them. (Cleaning up the trays/flower pots will clean up any diseases that might be harbored there – diseases that could affect your young seedlings. Use hot water, soap, and a dash of bleach.)

Be sure that, whatever you use, your planter has plenty of drainage holes! This is not negotiable!

For seeds, it's best to use a light seeding mix that is high in vermiculite, though not necessary. A regular "soilless" potting mix is fine. The seeding mix, which is more expensive, also is lighter and easier for newly-germinated seedlings to poke their little green heads through.

When I ran a greenhouse, I started my seedlings in trays and then transplanted them to six packs and four packs later on when they were big enough. For small windowsill operations, this won't be necessary. You can put some soil in a small Solo cup (with drainage holes poked into the bottom), stick two or three tomato seeds in there, and let 'em grow until they're big enough to transplant directly into the garden.

The tomato seeds will germinate more effectively if you have a heat mat under the cups or trays. This will warm the soil with dependable heat, allowing the seedlings to germinate more quickly and grow out more quickly. Just be sure to get a thermostat with the mats so you can adjust the temperature so you don't end up cooking your seeds.

How to plant tomato seeds

Fill your pots, cups, etc. with potting mix, leaving about a half-inch to an inch at the top. Poke two seeds into the middle, about a quarter-inch deep, and cover them. Two seeds are just insurance, just in case one doesn't sprout. When they get bigger, pinch out the wimpier seedling and let the larger one grow.

Gently pack the soil in around the seeds, as seed-to-soil contact is very important for good germination rates.

Sprinkle water on the soil, and keep the soil moist. Don't let it dry out, and don't let it get soggy all the time. Having the soil dry out will kill the seedlings, and constantly wet soil will rot them.

Now one way to keep the soil from drying out is to cover the trays or pots with plastic wrap. This is an easy way to keep the soil moist.

If you use plastic wrap, don't leave the trays in direct sunlight. One time I had the soil covered this way on one of my flats. I came in from one of my jobs and realized that it had been sitting in the sun all afternoon. I ran over and lifted up the plastic wrap – and steam puffed out. Those seeds were roasted!

Once the seeds germinate, though, be sure to remove the plastic wrap, and also have a small fan to keep the air circulating a little around them. Seedling are susceptible to a disease called "damping off" which is encouraged by poor air circulation.

Damping-off disease

I had a bout of damping-off disease in my greenhouse, and it was a mess. Damping-off is a fungal disease that causes newly-planted seedlings to keel over and melt away. It spreads out in a circle, as most funguses do (consider "fairy rings," which are circles of mushrooms on the forest floor), killing off seedlings as it spreads outward.

I haven't had damping-off before, since I keep stuff more on the dry side in the greenhouse, which the fungus doesn't like. However, we had cloudy, cold weather for a whole week, and my trays of seedlings, watered on a Sunday, would not dry out for the rest of the week. No sun, and I couldn't turn on the fans to pull the air through because it was too cold. Humidity was high. All the conditions were right for the fungus to strike.

Then the disease got into the snapdragons I'd just planted and started knocking them out everywhere. I called everyone I could think of for help. Then I took their advice, and it worked.

The best defense is a good offense. Keep a fan running at all times to keep the air circulating. You should feel the air moving through the whole room, but you don't have to turn it up so high that it blows the mice out from under the floor. Keep the plants spaced apart to let air move between them. The fungus likes high humidity and temperatures about 70 degrees. The fan keeps the humidity and temperature lower.

This will break your heart, but get rid of everything that's been infected by the fungus. Dump out the soil and the plants with them, and take the waste outside so spores won't reinfect the plants. As soon as you see the plant keel over, and you know it's not due to being underwatered, out it goes.

If it's a really valuable tray of seedlings, you might dig out the infected plants, isolate the tray from all the other plants, and try a soil drench of Captan fungicide (follow label directions). However, don't bank on saving the seedlings.

Hardening off the seedlings

Once the seedlings get big and husky, and once the weather warms up outside, it's time to harden off the seedlings so they can get acclimated to the weather outside. Plants do better if they have a little time to adjust to the cold temperatures, and the sun, and the wind.

About a week or two before you plan on planting them outside, start moving them outside for a little while. On the first couple of days, water them, then set them outside in the shade in a protected, warm area for an hour or two, then bring them back inside. Then slowly increase exposure to the sun and wind, leaving them out three hours, or four. Then, when you are close to planting time, leave them outside overnight several times (but only if the temperature is supposed to stay over 50 degrees all night).

While you're hardening them off, keep an eye on them to make sure they're not wilting or drying out.

When they're inside, reduce the amount of water you give them, and don't fertilize them until you plant them in the garden.

Don't worry if you miss a day, and don't stress about "not doing it right." Plants are often tougher than we give them credit for, and often there's no real "right way" or "wrong way." Sometimes regular life gets in the way, so if you can't put your seedlings out every single day, it's okay, just put them out when you can.

ABOUT THE AUTHOR

Melinda R. Cordell worked in most all aspects of horticulture – garden centers, wholesale greenhouses, as a landscape designer, and finally as city horticulturist, where she took care of 20+ gardens around the city. She lives in northwest Missouri with her husband and kids, the best little family that ever walked the earth.

My first book, **Courageous Women of the Civil War: Soldiers, Spies, Medics, and More** was published by Chicago Review Press in August 2016. This was a series of profiles of women who fought or cared for the wounded during the Civil War. I found stories about some of the women that had not been seen for decades.

Immediately after, I self-published a short stack of gardening books, a short-story collection called **Angel in the Whirlwind**, and **Butterfly Chaos**, which I worked on with Gary Schmidt and Mary Logue at Hamline.

My first gardening book is **Don't Throw in the Trowel: Vegetable Gardening Month by Month**. That was followed up by the rosarian-approved **Rose to the Occasion: An Easy-Growing Guide to Rose Gardening**, and recently, **If You're a Tomato, I'll Ketchup With You: Tomato Gardening Tips and Tricks**. And now here is my Perennials book!

My newest novel is **Those Black Wings**, about a shy gal who runs screaming from love – and then gets in way, way over her head.

Be sure to recommend my books to any of your gardener friends (and even your gardener enemies).

Follow me on Twitter at @rosefiend for garden stuff and lots of other stuff.

If you like this book, please leave a review on my Amazon or Goodreads page. Reviews help me get more readers.

Thanks so much for reading.
melindacordell.com

Made in the USA
Lexington, KY
21 October 2017